PANORAMA OF WORLD ART

ART OF THE EARLY MIDDLE AGES

ART OF THE EARLY MIDDLE AGES

Text by FRANÇOIS SOUCHAL

With an Introduction by Hans H. Hofstätter

HARRY N. ABRAMS, INC. / NEW YORK / LONDON

Text translated from the French by
Ronald Millen

Introduction translated from the German by
Robert Erich Wolf

Library of Congress Catalog Card Number: 68-27428

Harry N. Abrams, Incorporated, New York
Printed in West Germany. Bound in the Netherlands

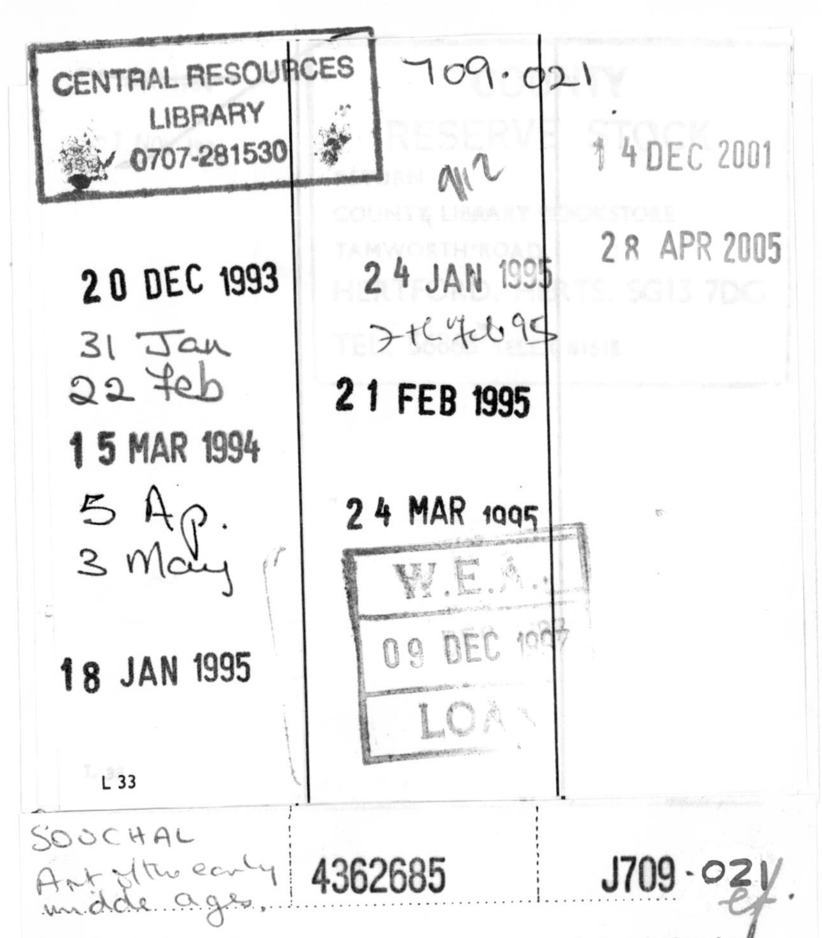
CENTRAL RESOURCES
LIBRARY
0707-281530
709·021
COUNTY
RESERVE STOCK
14 DEC 2001
28 APR 2005
20 DEC 1993
24 JAN 1995
31 Jan
22 Feb
21 FEB 1995
15 MAR 1994
5 Ap.
3 May
24 MAR 1995
W.E.A.
09 DEC 1997
LOAN
18 JAN 1995
L 33

TRUST AND FEAR NOT

Contents

Introduction

by Hans H. Hofstätter

This book is about the artistic achievements of the Early Middle Ages, and the religious and political interconnections of the time in so far as they may bc reflected in the arts. The period covers some two hundred and fifty years, from the beginning of the eleventh century to around the middle of the thirteenth. Art historians call the style of this period Romanesque, but they do not all agree on when and where it began. Its end is much clearer: in its last years it became a transitional style leading into the Gothic. In Germanic regions it is thought of as a new style which followed the Ottonian art of the tenth century. In the rest of Europe, most notably in France, Spain, and Italy, the beginnings of the style are generally viewed differently, as an uninterrupted growth out of the earliest medieval art, that art which reached its first climax in the ninth century under the Carolingians. The argument for this is based on the idea that, in Romanesque art, all the diverse strands of the earlier period were brought together, clarified, and developed further in a systematic manner. From that standpoint, it follows that Carolingian art itself can be taken as the start of the Romanesque. Some French scholars do, in fact, speak of the Carolingian and Ottonian epochs as "the first Romanesque art" (though they date its beginnings with considerable flexibility) and term the period treated in the present book as "the second Romanesque art."

Despite all the accidents of time and history which any systematic classification is bound to ignore when applied to ages which once were quick with life and now seem so remote from us, the limits imposed on the period in this book seem justified. Within the time it treats, developments ran their course and new factors made their presence felt, and those made up a whole clearly different from anything that preceded or followed it. This is true in all its aspects, whether political history, the way of thinking about the world, the organization of society, its theology and natural sciences, architecture, sculpture, painting, poetry, or music. So complex, so rich, was the period that, in a book on art, we can do no more than suggest those nonartistic factors which, in one way or another, played a significant part.

Politically, the Early Middle Ages were a time of reshuffling of the relations between the great powers which controlled life throughout Europe. Emperor and Pope, once joined together in supporting and furthering the idea of Western civilization, now became rivals in a struggle that reached its climax in the dispute over the right of investiture of bishops, which pitted Emperor Henry IV against Pope Gregory VII in 1076. It was also the age of the Crusades, the most enormous political and religious blunder in utilization of men and forces ever committed by the Western world. And yet, something of infinite value came out of that foolhardy venture. Because of it, both the spiritual and the economic horizons of the entire Occident underwent an extraordinary broadening. Into what had been until then a closed world were introduced new stimuli from abroad, and these churned European thought and learning into a ferment, forcing them into new channels. Finally, it was the epoch during which German Imperial power gradually disintegrated while, at the same time, the French Kingdom grew steadily stronger, with the result that political and intellectual concepts throughout Europe became displaced in the direction of France.

Sociologically, the Early Middle Ages brought in a great broadening of the power of the nobility (which was to be of significant consequence in the times to come), while the lower classes remained unaffected to any measurable degree. The earliest medieval times, under the Carolingians and Ottonians, were dominated by an aristocracy which had grown out of the old Teutonic tribal leaders and the Roman senatorial families. It was that group which had the monopoly of both ecclesiastical and secular positions, and which laid down the laws and administered justice. Conservative to the hilt, they viewed themselves as the protectors of tradition and custom. But, as things developed, such a small body of nobles no longer sufficed to govern vastly extended territories, to administer them in peace, or to defend them in war. The base of the social pyramid supporting the king or the emperor had therefore to be made ever broader. In order to maintain a trained body of administrators and an experienced army, it became necessary to purchase the loyalty of the individuals in charge of them with grants of land, guarantees of immunity, and special privileges; and these, as time went on, were handed down from generation to generation. This meant, however, that territories which initially had been the exclusive property of the king now, in fact, changed hands and were held by his subordinates. In this way the powers of the ruler himself were diminished. In every sense, then, the feudal lords exercised supreme power in their own territories. True, they were sworn to loyalty and good faith toward the king or emperor, especially when it came to military support, but they could also influence decisively the political activity of the crown, which consequently became more and more dependent on their good will. Conflicts were inevitable, and these became increasingly more numerous and more bitter.

As earlier, alongside the sovereign's court, intellectual activity remained in the hands of the monasteries, above all those of the Benedictine and Cistercian orders. By founding tributary monasteries throughout Europe, those orders were responsible for a feverish activity in building, the like of which we can scarcely envisage today. To them also we owe whatever has survived of Romanesque culture. Through them, and through their missionary zeal, the religious life of the people was so completely determined that what we know about the ordinary men of the time has to do largely with their relations with the Church—far more, in any case, than with their political life as affected by the activities of the nobility. A word of caution, therefore, about the one-sidedness of our information about the life of the time: it cannot fail to distort any conclusions we may draw about such intellectual and personal attitudes of the people as were not directly determined by Church or State. As for how they really felt and thought about religion, we can glean something of that from the great sanctuaries which attracted hordes of pilgrims often from remote corners of Europe; and the religious images before which the people prayed offer us something like a concentrate of the spiritual forces of the age.

The three greatest pilgrimage centers in the Early Middle Ages were Jerusalem, Rome, and Santiago de Compostela in northwestern Spain. As far back as Charlemagne, an agreement had been made with the Islamic rulers to guarantee the well-being and safety of Western pilgrims in the Holy Land. Despite the trials and perils of the long journey, the places where Christ lived and died were visited constantly: no less than six times did the holy man John of Parma make the pilgrimage to Jerusalem. When, later, Caliph Hakim set aside the pacts with the West and permitted the Christian settlements in the Holy Land to be destroyed, there was a storm of indignation everywhere in Europe and, at the same time, a determination to preserve the sacred places of Christendom. This was the pretext for the many Crusades which followed, and one of the results of those military ventures was that those who had been abroad returned with new knowledge which gave a fresh impetus to the architecture of Europe. However, the exchanges in both directions were lively, there was an active give and take, and today scholars debate about just which architectural forms were really imported into Europe from the East. Be that as it may, one type of construction at least, and one which was repeated over and over in the West, testifies to the impact made by the East on the Crusaders: innumerable chapels or royal burial places were built in imitation of the Holy Sepulcher, the rotunda over the tomb of Christ in Jerusalem, and many of these were designed as thank offerings for a safe return to the homeland.

Romanesque architecture was also influenced by the pilgrimages to Rome, the holiest place in the Christian West, where so many of the early martyrs had died and were buried. From Rome vast numbers of relics were brought back to the North to be preserved in costly shrines made specially for them. No less important were the catacombs, for they were taken as models for the crypts which were built under the choirs of churches as a sort of church beneath a church, or which were designed as passageways with chapel-like additions to house the precious relics, past which the faithful were invited to parade in solemn processions. Such churches took the place of the great pilgrimage centers for those not often able, or entirely unable, to make the long journey to Rome or the Holy Land; and they made it possible for thousands to visit repeatedly and venerate the transplanted relics, which had, as it were, acquired rights of citizenship in a foreign land, along with the saints with whom they were associated and who became the patrons of the local church or town.

One of the chief places to attract multitudes of pilgrims was the tomb of the Apostle James in Santiago de Compostela. Legend attributed to him the Spanish victory over the Moors, and so he lived on in popular piety as intercessor for the reconquest of Spain from the rule of Islam and as the saint who would guarantee good fortune to the Crusaders in their reconquest of the Holy Land. The Romanesque cathedral in Santiago de Compostela was begun before 1077 to replace an earlier, smaller church which had proved inadequate to accommodate the hordes of pilgrims. The choir and transept were consecrated in 1105, and by around 1130 the nave was completed up to the west front, on which work still continued. Santiago became the most important ecclesiastical building on Spanish soil, closely related architecturally to Saint-Sernin in Toulouse.

Almost more important than the terminal points of the pilgrimages were the roads which led to them from various places in the North. Along those roads grew up important monastic foundations, which provided shelter for the crowds who visited these holy places as way stations on their pilgrimages and who not infrequently rewarded them with rich treasures. Those monasteries also had artistic links: itinerant troops of masons and sculptors traveled from one to the other, and today we can still trace their routes, through similarities in style, across great distances. One of the main highways for pilgrims and artists alike began at Saint-Denis outside Paris and led through Orléans to Tours; there it joined another road beginning in Chartres and continued by way of Poitiers to Ostabat in the Pyrenees. At Ostabat it linked up with two other pilgrimage routes, one which led from Vézelay through Périgueux, the other from Le Puy through Conques and Moissac. From that point the mass of pilgrims from many places all traveled together by way of Roncesvalles, Burgos, and León. At Puente la Reina their ranks were swelled by other pilgrims who had made their way from Arles through Toulouse and Somport. The monasteries which were the pilgrims' way stations provided not only food and lodging but also protection from the highwaymen who infested the roads. But, besides these great pilgrimages which set entire populations in movement across Europe, there were many smaller pilgrimages to local sanctuaries. Nor were the monasteries and churches along the great routes mere halting places. They too were goals for pilgrims, and each had its own special importance. They were visited not only by those who continued their journey to Santiago but by others who came to address their prayers to their own personal intercessors. In this way, the popular faith of the time gave rise to an immense activity aimed at personal salvation, and it must be understood in this light.

Not only the great territorial holdings of the monasteries, and their greater or lesser independence of the secular powers, but also their awareness of what a great spiritual ally they had in the masses of the people, made it possible for those ecclesiastical foundations to weather their own crises, centered around proposals for reform, which often set them at odds with the temporal rulers and with the practice and traditions of the Church. In 910 a monastery was founded at Cluny in Burgundy. From it there came a wave of monastic reform, which aimed to free the Church from the control of the laity and to invert the long-standing subordination of the powers of God to those of man. The monastery at Cluny was founded by Duke William of

Aquitaine with funds drawn entirely from his own family estate. He bequeathed it formally to the Princes of the Apostles, Peter and Paul, and placed it under the direct protection of the Pope while, at the same time, forestalling any possibility of the Pope's profiting from it in any way. This form of endowment was, to say the least, revolutionary. It broke with all established usage. Always before, the founder and his heirs had retained rights to the revenues of a monastery, but in the charter William expressly ruled out all further claims, including those of his own heirs. Further, in a clause guaranteeing immunity, the king, the count, the bishop, and even the Pope were warned not to attempt to seize the monastery, under pain of answering for their misdeed at the Last Judgment. So, for the first time in history, there came into being a completely independent monastic community. The first abbot, Bruno, demanded a rigorous application of the monastic rules of Saint Benedict. Under his direction, the monastery became not only economically self-sufficient but also independent of the jurisdiction of both the bishop and the Church; after him, every abbot himself named his successor.

This dynamic reform was associated with a new liturgical spirit. In the daily life of the monks, prayer played a much greater role than ever before. Group prayer was doubled in scope to become a kind of ceaseless, continuous worship. Among other innovations, prayers for the dead became a permanent feature of the liturgy of the Mass and thereby fulfilled a true and deep-seated need of popular piety, renewing the ancient pagan tradition of ancestor worship.

The monastic reform at Cluny quickly had repercussions elsewhere. In the German Imperial territory, however, it met with opposition and was only adopted after the decline of the Ottonian dynasty. This was because the abbots and abbesses were often related to the Imperial family, a situation not likely to encourage attempts at autonomy. Nevertheless, elsewhere the ecclesiastical authorities and bishops did call in Cluniac monks to reform the monasteries under their control. From time to time a number of foundations were consolidated into a single congregation subject to one central monastery. Something between 1,200 and 1,450 monasteries became directly subordinate to Cluny, and another 1,600 monastic communities joined the movement of reform. The abbot of Cluny became Abbot of the Abbots, to whom all monks and all other monasteries either directly or indirectly owed obedience. But such rigorous centralization, which stamped an entire age with the mark of monastic power, could not fail to bring with it certain risks. Such a gigantic union of some three thousand communities simply could not be governed properly by a single abbot. As a consequence, alongside Cluny there sprang up other reform movements whose effectiveness, however, was not tied to any particular territory. In Lotharingian Verdun a separate reform was launched, which spread to Flanders and Germany; another began, soon after Cluny's, in Brogne near Namur; and there were still others in southern Italy and at Canterbury. Closest to the particular policy of Cluny was the reform that took place at Gorze near Metz in 933, and this had greater influence in the Ottonian Imperial territories because it placed more emphasis on a balance between Church and State in a feudal order, shying away from all suggestions of monastic monopoly and centralization. Nevertheless, in the last years of the eleventh century, the Cluniac reform gained a foothold in the monastery of Hirsau in the Black Forest, whence sprang a reform movement which played an important role in the struggle over the right of investiture.

To make reality of a program of the scope which Cluny proposed required new and more spacious buildings. Continuous prayer—which meant that every priest had to say Mass every day—not only brought about an extension of the liturgy but also a new type of sanctuary in the church, the so-called "Cluniac choir." In this, the main choir was preceded by an aisled forechoir two bays long and having accessory areas to the sides. The main choir was flanked by two narrow subsidiary choirs and terminated in an apse and ambulatory, from which radiated a ring of apsidal chapels. The arms of the transepts were likewise extended into apses and chapels. This proliferation of chapels was required in order to make it possible for a large number of monk-priests to perform the daily sacrifice of the Mass. At Cluny itself, this elaborate arrangement of the choir was completed by a massive nave, made necessary because the innumerable subsidiary monasteries often gathered for joint prayer in the chief church of the order. From a nineteenth-century sketch of the now-destroyed church we gather that the nave was double-aisled and that there were two transepts, seven towers, and an aisled atrium at the west end. The result was a church which was the most important architectural achievement of its time outside of the Ottonian Imperial regions, and its influence reached far into the Romanesque era.

The most significant reform movement after that of Cluny was initiated by Bernard of Clairvaux (1091–1153), who in 1115 created the Cistercian monastery of Clairvaux as a dependency of the abbey of Cîteaux. Bernard is one of the great key figures of medieval faith. Irresistible as a preacher, his sermons attracted pilgrims from the most remote places. The Catholic Church ranks him among the great intercessors of the Middle Ages, one who set a model of style and content for personal prayer and whose influence endured for many centuries. His veneration of Jesus and Mary, which laid the ground for the mysticism of the Late Middle Ages, was nevertheless strictly rooted in the teachings of the early Fathers of the Church. He was critical of any compromise with worldly values which might tempt the Church from its spiritual functions. He thundered against the wealth of Cluny and criticized the worldly and political pretensions of the Pope, although in the conflict over investiture he stood solidly with the Papacy. His declared hostility to cultural pursuits and his rejection of any scientific foundation for theology in favor of a private, intuitive experience of God exercised a profoundly fertile influence on his times.

In the same way as Cluny's reforms were of great consequence in the development of monastic architecture, so too were Bernard's directives decisive for the construction and furnishing of monastic churches. He spurned virtually all decoration as superfluous, but, in compensation, called for the highest standards of craftsmanship in the basic construction. To his mind, painstaking workmanship in the hewing out of masonry blocks or the carving of columns and capitals was an ample alternative to the employment of unnecessary decorative elements. What is more, in churches built according to his prescriptions, there are no towers, a simple turret being deemed sufficient for the single bell needed to summon the faithful to worship. The choir is generally closed off simply; in place of stained glass, the windows are clear panes or, at most, grisaille; there are no elaborately carved capitals and no wall paintings. Well into Gothic times the Cistercians continued to obey Bernard's insistence on simplicity, and they applied it even to the architectural ideas of that more complex age. Their Gothic churches are sparing in the use of vaulting and tracery, do not employ the triforium to articulate the lateral walls, and, on the exterior, limit the buttressing to what is strictly necessary for functional purposes.

We have seen to what extent the basic structure of Romanesque churches was influenced by religious and liturgical practice, how certain theological postulates became directly responsible for the invention of certain architectural forms, and why a desire for autonomy—the defense of which, in some cases, even became urgent when a church was located in a politically turbulent region—led to the designing of religious buildings as something like fortresses of God. Outside, there were solid, impregnable walls, and above the walls rose majestic groups of towers. The interior was rigorously divided into separate places for worship, and nearby lay peaceful cloisters inviting meditation and inward concentration. It was in these forms that Romanesque architecture expressed the security of the Christian faith in a world which threatened it from without. That threat was not only political, it was also spiritual. In Romanesque architectonic sculpture, demons were depicted, for the first time, as ever-present threats to the faith which every Christian was called upon to combat. There are violent illustrations of the excommunication and damning of the Evil Ones who, on church portals, are depicted as horrible misshapen animals, or on pillars as masses of beasts heaped up and intertwining, or forcibly confined outside the gates of the sanctuary, or protestingly chained together in the form of the Cross.

In the Romanesque era, the Church covered the Occident with ten thousand such citadels against Evil. Never before had Europe known such a furor of building, and this constitutes yet another factor which distinguishes that age from the Carolingian and Ottonian periods which preceded it. Quite literally astonishing is the diversity of architectural solutions found for ground plans, though the forms remained substantially those taken over from Antiquity: the basilica and the central-plan church. But unlike the periods which preceded and followed it, the development of ecclesiastical architecture in the Romanesque was not based on imitation of any particular previous model and its local variants. The opposite was true. In a number of places throughout Europe, right from the outset, individual styles of construction were worked out. These then became known and imitated in wider areas, and their diffusion was determined by certain specific geographical relationships, such as the pilgrimage routes. Only later did those many individual stimuli intercross and lead gradually to a common Romanesque style, though even then they never set aside their particular local traditions. Another distinction of the Romanesque from the periods preceding it is, therefore, this multifarious development from a number of local expressions.

One of the most conspicuous problems of Romanesque architecture concerned the construction of vaults. The problem was approached in the most diverse ways, and its solutions were equally diverse. It was centuries since anyone anywhere in the West had understood or could remember how the great vaulted edifices of ancient Rome had been built. Only the Byzantine East remembered and carried on the tradition. The Early Christian basilicas, and the churches which followed them, were limited to flat roofing or open rafterwork. For a long time those monasteries where the principles of reform opposed architectural extravagance did not venture beyond that primitive solution—not until the secrets of vaulting great edifices had become known thoughout the West. The earliest example of a vaulted interior was the cathedral of Speyer. Between 1030 and 1061 its Early Romanesque nave was roofed over with a flat ceiling. Later, around 1100, after the outer walls had been reinforced, it was provided with a groined vault. But there as elsewhere, wherever vaulting was attempted, it involved a radical change in the character of the supporting walls, for the simple reason that there is a great difference between a wall that is weighted down directly perpendicularly by a flat timberwork ceiling and one that must bear the additional and not inconsiderable outward thrust of a vault. The solution arrived at was a rhythmic articulation of both the interior and exterior of the church, the points of concentrated thrust being especially reinforced by massive piers. Characteristically, however, such rhythmic articulation—alternation of supports in the interior, reinforcement of engaged shafts on the exterior—had already been worked out and applied even before builders began to concern themselves with vaulting. This was quite simply because of the need to divide the interior space in a way quite opposed to the undifferentiated arcaded naves of Early Christian basilicas, and because of the desire to articulate that space into successive, regular bays. The final consequence of this architectural conception was the introduction of the technique of vaulting. In the last phase of the Gothic, when that style was in dissolution, this basic conception would once again be abandoned.

Romanesque architecture is composed of blocklike, articulated bays that follow one another in a rhythmic manner, often comprising elements derived from earlier forms that are now modified and combined at will. This is true also of the repertory of images used in Romanesque sculpture and painting. These are conceived as something entirely different from man himself, something wholly opposite to him. In contemplating those images and worshiping before them, man has no choice except to forget his own existence. They do not invite identification or empathy, man cannot recognize himself in them as he can in the Gothic images which came later. With them, there is an unmistakable gulf between the worshiper and the image he venerates. In sculpture, as in architecture, the change from Romanesque to Gothic was fluid and imprecise, as indeed were also the beginnings of Romanesque sculpture itself. What we find already fully stamped with its own character in the eleventh and twelfth centuries was the product of a lengthy preparation, anticipated long before by a few surviving masterworks, most of which date from the Ottonian period. Among such forms are the Madonna enthroned with the Infant Jesus and the monumental images of Christ crucified. In general, however, Romanesque sculpture and painting are characterized by a rejection of the antiquating tendencies which had been the decisive factors in the Carolingian and Ottonian styles. Those tendencies had comprised spatial and corporeal illusionism, the use of *contrapposto* in depicting the human figure, and decorative forms derived from nature. These were things learned from Antique models, but to them the Ottonian period had added a deeper, more inward spiritual significance which tended more and more to supplant the natural forms. The trend toward spirituality reached its culmination in the Romanesque. There, everything suggesting natural configurations was rigorously subordinated to symbolism. Nothing was envisaged as a part of natural Creation but only as an abstract sign denoting a transcendental content. In painting, the personifications of Christian faith were depicted as if detached from all human sentiment, as triumphant symbols throning over altars, portals, the conches of apses, or the walls of the House of God. In earlier art, the spatial depth in which figures seemed to take on a common movement was the binding link. Now that link was no more than the flat surface on which these symbolic figures were painted. The figures took their places in a composition determined by the surface area to be covered, not by the laws of spatial illusion. They were simply placed side by side or one above the other, and this accounts for their ornamental character. But such compositions must not be misinterpreted as "decorative," because the prime factor remained always their spiritual significance.

Sculpture was conceived in relation to architecture. The sacred events of Scripture and legend were represented on the capitals of basilicas and cloisters; statues of prophets and Apostles were inseparable parts of the piers and walls of cloisters, tribunes, ambulatories, and crypts. From 1100 on, church façades were more and more adorned with reliefs, until they became at last complete screens of carved images. On such façades the old notion survived that everything must be thought of in terms of parable. Already in Ottonian times the west front of a church was seen as a bastion raised against the spirits of Hell. The consecrated images on the façade barred the enemy spirits from entering into the sanctuary, and there, outside, the demons' power was foiled as surely as was that of those other demons who, trapped inside the church, were shown chained to pedestals or crushed under columns.

In the course of the twelfth century, these abstract, symbolic representations gradually came to be animated from within by traits that could only come from spontaneous observation of nature. From this there grew a new and thoroughgoing transformation in style which led to the Gothic and, thereby, to new ways of thought, to a new organization and broadening of the old repertory of images and of their relationship to architecture. Depending on the role which the individual centers of art had played in the Romanesque, their transition to the Gothic took place more or less rapidly or slowly. The fact is, the Gothic originated in a region where, as far as we can tell now, there had been no particularly significant Romanesque architecture, and it grew there from Romanesque roots contributed by other regions—Normandy above all—but with an entirely new spiritual conception. The Gothic spread most rapidly in those regions whose art had not come into its own until toward the end of the Romanesque era, which meant that there was a virtually continuous transition between the two styles. Other regions seemed almost to repulse the Gothic, and those were regions where Romanesque creations had founded an exemplary and sturdy tradition which seemed destined to remain valid forever. In those places, Romanesque style lingered on in decline for almost another three-quarters of a century, and even when they finally adopted Gothic structures and forms, the native tradition left its mark on them. From this point of view, the argument advanced in the opening lines of this essay is further corroborated: that the Romanesque was the first period since Antiquity in which the separate peoples and localities found their way to an art which expressed their own special way of life, their own unique character.

South façade and bell tower, basilica of Saint-Sernin, Toulouse. Late twelfth–thirteenth centuries

The Christ in Majesty (page 13), wedged into a mandorla between the symbols of the four Evangelists, is one of seven large marble reliefs which decorate the choir of the great pilgrimage church of Saint-Sernin. It is a precious heritage from the very beginning of the great period of Romanesque sculpture and from one of its main centers of diffusion, Languedoc. In style, it has much in common with the ivory reliefs on the covers of Gospel lectionaries of the time.

Saint-Sernin in Toulouse ranked among the principal churches on one of the great pilgrimage routes to Santiago de Compostela. The spacious choir with its ambulatory, together with the vast transept, permitted the free movement of the crowds of pilgrims who came to venerate the relics of Saint Saturninus, who had brought Christianity to Aquitania. The great church may have been begun as early as c. 1060, but the upper stories of the tower were not finished until the thirteenth century. Toulouse itself was one of the most important centers of Romanesque architecture and sculpture.

Women Holding the Signs of the Lion and the Ram. Mid-twelfth century. Marble relief, 53 × 26¾″. Musée des Augustins, Toulouse

The meaning of this low relief, which comes from Saint-Sernin, remains an enigma, for influence from classical Antiquity is paired here with traditional Eastern forms. It is not without significance that figures with very similar iconography and style are found also at Santiago de Compostela. This testifies to the existence of a school of sculpture active on both sides of the Pyrenees (see page 237).

The Feast of Herod, capital from twinned columns, formerly in the cloisters of Saint-Étienne, Toulouse. c. mid-twelfth century. Stone, $12^5/_8 \times 22''$. Musée des Augustins, Toulouse

This capital has as its subject the story of John the Baptist. Its left face shows the feast of Herod, with the head of the Baptist being presented on a platter to Salome, who hands it to Herodias. This vestige of the now-destroyed cloisters of Saint-Étienne reveals, in its feeling for composition and its effort to capture something picturesque and animated, how the sculpture of Languedoc grew ever richer in the course of the twelfth century.

The scene from the life of Saint Matthew shows him in dispute with Hirtacus, King of Ethiopia. It is evidence ▶ of the far-reaching influence of French Romanesque art, which was carried abroad by the Crusaders.

Saint Matthew and the King of Ethiopia, capital from the former basilica of Nazareth. c. 1187. Franciscan monastery, Nazareth, Israel

Christ in Glory. 1020–21. Marble lintel carved in low relief. Saint-Genis-des-Fontaines (Pyrénées-Orientales)

This is a work of considerable importance in the history of Western sculpture, since it marks the return of the low relief into art, for all that its technique is still very rudimentary and its forms naïve and awkward. It presents a motif very frequent in Romanesque art, that of Christ in Glory with the Apostles lined up on either side under arcades. Here the lintel is framed by a frieze of stylized foliage.

Interior of the church, former abbey of Escaladieu (Hautes-Pyrénées). Consecrated 1160 ▶

The Cistercians, who adopted the austerely simple forms of the Romanesque, built here a church with a broad pointed barrel vault whose transverse arches, along with the side chapels with their transverse vaulting, set up a rhythmic movement.

Last Judgment, tympanum of the church of Sainte-Foy, Conques (Aveyron). Second quarter of twelfth century

The abbey of Sainte-Foy at Conques was one of the most important halting places in the mountains on the route to Santiago de Compostela. The church contained the celebrated relics of the young virgin martyr Saint Foy, and there too thousands of pilgrims could contemplate the great Last Judgment on the tympanum, one of the most complete in all of the Romanesque. The style of the rather thickset figures on this grandiose low relief is related to that of the Auvergne, one of the richest areas of Romanesque art.

Detail of upper part of the nave, ▶ Sainte-Foy, Conques. Eleventh century

Here we see the powerful structure of this pilgrimage church whose narrow, shaftlike nave is covered by a barrel vault and flanked by aisles surmounted by a spacious gallery which, above each bay, opens up in a double arch. Light pours in through the galleries and also through the cupola over the crossing.

◀ The reliquary statue of Saint Foy is the most precious possession of the former abbey. It took its present form in the course of many periods. The gold head undoubtedly goes back to Byzantine times, and the gold sheathing of the body, constructed around a wooden core, dates as far back as the end of the ninth century. Part of the decoration was done in the tenth century, and it was added to and modified throughout the Middle Ages. This is not truly a statue but rather a reliquary designed to enshrine the head of the martyr.

Below is another famous piece in the abbey's treasury. Legend has it that Charlemagne himself gave it to the abbey. There has been a great deal of dispute, with no positive results, as to why this reliquary was made in such a strange form.

◀ Reliquary statue of Saint Foy. Ninth–tenth centuries. Wooden body covered by plaques of gold leaf, ornamented with bands of filigree, enamels, cabochons, and engraved gems, and with eyes of glass paste, height $33^1/_2$''. Treasury, church of Sainte-Foy, Conques

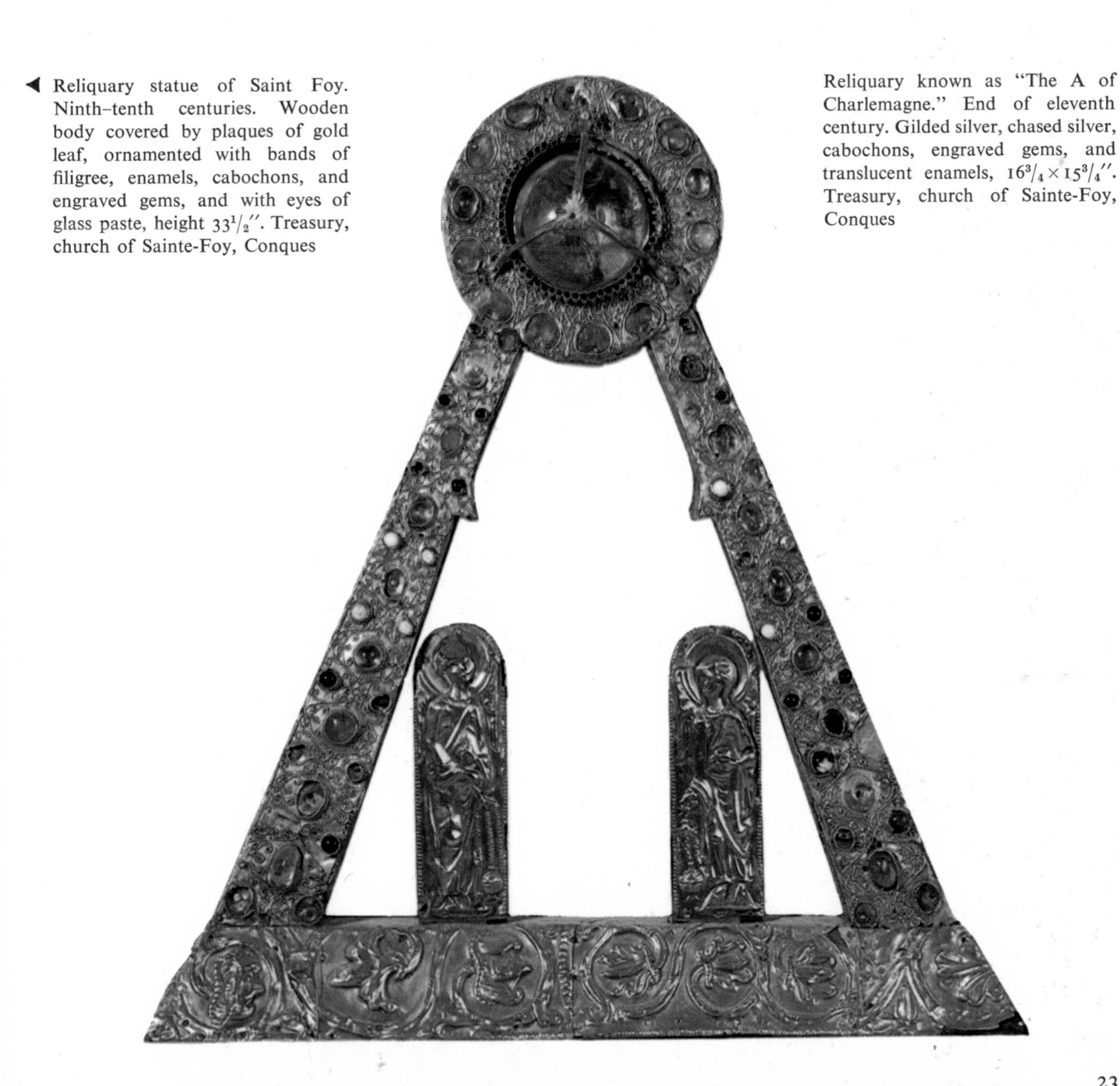

Reliquary known as "The A of Charlemagne." End of eleventh century. Gilded silver, chased silver, cabochons, engraved gems, and translucent enamels, $16^3/_4 \times 15^3/_4$''. Treasury, church of Sainte-Foy, Conques

The donjon of Houdan (Seine-et-Oise). c. 1130 ▶

The keep is all that remains of the fortress built by Amaury de Monfort (1105–37), and it is a rare example of military architecture of the period. It has an unusual design, being circular and flanked by round turrets, and is one of the earliest instances of a round tower. Its diameter is some fifty feet, and that of the turrets approximately thirteen feet.

Saint Gauzelin, Bishop of Toul (922–62), founded the abbey of Bouxières, where, until the French Revolution, these objects which had belonged to him were preserved. These two liturgical vessels are as remarkable for their harmony of design and proportions as for the delicacy of their execution.

Chalice and paten of Saint Gauzelin. Tenth century. Chalice in gold with filigree, enamel, pearls, emeralds, and other gems, height $5^1/_2$″. Paten in gold and silver, with filigree, pearls, cabochons, and enamel, diameter $5^7/_8$″. Treasury of the cathedral, Nancy (Meurthe-et-Moselle)

Last Judgment, tympanum of the former priory of Saint-Pierre, Carennac (Lot). Second quarter of twelfth century. Stone, 7′ 2½″ × 14′ 4½″

The Last Judgment is represented here according to the Apocalypse, with Christ in Glory in the center surrounded by the symbols of the Evangelists and attended by the Apostles, who converse among themselves in pairs. The tympanum is divided into rectangular compartments, much as in altar frontals made of precious metals or, again, as in ivory coffers from the Orient. Its geometrical and plantlike decorative motifs also suggest influence from the Orient. Stylistically, the work belongs to the Languedoc school of sculpture.

Last Judgment, tympanum of the former Benedictine abbey of Beaulieu (Corrèze). First half of twelfth century. Stone, 13′ 5½″ × 19′ 3½″

In this great Last Judgment there are certain unusual elements which were destined to have some influence later, such as the representation of the Instruments of the Passion held by angels. The lower tiers are filled with an extraordinary procession of swarming monsters who typify the evil forces which Christ the Judge has overthrown. Despite a certain confusion in organization, this splendid low relief, teeming with powerful and strange figures, is one of the masterpieces of Romanesque sculpture in southwestern France.

Façade of Saint-Michel d'Aiguilhe, Le Puy (Haute-Loire). Eleventh–twelfth centuries

Perched on the summit of a rocky peak, this tiny church testifies to the influence of Mozarabic art, an influence which spread out along the pilgrimage routes, on which Le Puy was an important stopping place. This is easily recognizable in the special form of the trefoiled horseshoe arch which decorates the portal, as well as in the play of interlacing plant motifs. At Le Puy, a considerable part was played by Byzantine influence also, as is seen in the hieratic dignity of the sculptured and painted figures and in the imitation of mosaic work.

Assumption of the Virgin, capital in the choir of Notre-Dame-du-Port, Clermont-Ferrand (Puy-de-Dôme). Mid-twelfth century

The Assumption of the Virgin, as represented here, follows a pseudepigraphic Gospel. An angel blows a trumpet and the Gate of Paradise swings open to receive the Virgin Mary. This is a good example of the narrative style of the sculptors of Auvergne who, typically, gave to their figures a heavy, squat form and crowded the entire capital with figures and accessory motifs.

The Loire region and the west of France are particularly rich in Romanesque wall paintings. The rectangular choir at Brinay is completely covered with scenes of the childhood of Christ, painted in two zones. Here we see the angel bidding Joseph to depart, followed by the flight itself. There is little variety in the colors of the painting, which are predominantly red and yellow ocher, but the somewhat stiff drawing is not lacking in a certain dignity. This is one of the most complete cycles of wall paintings that has come down to us, and it is only some fifty years since the whitewash which had hidden it for centuries was removed.

The Flight into Egypt. Mid-twelfth century. Wall painting, 69 × 94″. Church of Saint-Aignan, Brinay (Cher)

The Taking of Christ in the Garden of Gethsemane. Beginning of twelfth century. Wall painting, 67 × 94½″. Church of Saint-Martin-de-Vic, Nohant-Vicq (Indre)

The choir of the little church of Vic is entirely covered by a remarkably well preserved ensemble of paintings set one above the other on the walls. All the work is obviously by the same hand. The main cycle is devoted to the Life of Christ, though a certain number of scenes are drawn from the Apocryphal books. The color has very little variation, the drawing is summary, contrasts of relief are lacking, and the figures themselves are inexpressive. Yet the spirited narrative and the artist's feeling for movement and for storytelling give a great deal of life to these paintings, as here where we see Saint Peter cutting off Malchus' ear.

Façade of the former town hall of Saint-Antonin-du-Gard (Tarn-et-Garonne). Twelfth century

There are very few Romanesque civil edifices remaining in France. The former town hall of Saint-Antonin was once the dwelling of a local noble family named Archambault. However, even in a building like this, intended for domestic use, religious art was not absent: of the two pillars which interrupt the colonnade of the middle story, one is sculpted into a King Solomon, the other into a Temptation of Adam and Eve.

Remains of the abbey church of Saints-Pierre-et-Paul, Cluny (Saône-et-Loire). c. 1100 ▶

This fragment of an arm of the transept is all that survives of what was once the greatest church of Christendom, the mother church of a powerful monastic movement.

◀ *Rotta Player (Allegory of a Gregorian Mode)*, capital from the former abbey of Cluny. Beginning of twelfth century. $33^1/_2 \times 31^1/_2''$. Former flour mill, abbey of Cluny

The Mystic Mill, capital in the abbey church of the Madeleine, Vézelay (Yonne). Second quarter of twelfth century

The connection between the Old and the New Testaments is presented symbolically on this capital: the grain of the Old Testament passes through the Mystic Mill to become the flour of the Gospels.

◀ The musicians on the four sides of this capital symbolize the basic modes of Gregorian chant as used in the liturgy. This noble and vigorous style set a model for Burgundian artists.

◀ Nave, abbey church of the Madeleine, Vézelay. Begun 1120

Guardian of the venerable relics of Mary Magdalen, Vézelay was once a famed place of pilgrimage. To its daringly conceived Romanesque nave a Gothic choir was added at the end of the twelfth century. Long neglected, the church was saved from ruin in the nineteenth century by Viollet-le-Duc's restorations.

The illustration below shows a fragment of a low relief—all that survives of the sculpture on the lateral portals of the cathedral of Autun. The Fall of Man is strikingly represented by the naked Eve gliding among leaves while picking the apple, and the result is sculpture of a powerful dynamic equilibrium.

Eve, from the cathedral of Saint-Lazare, Autun (Saône-et-Loire). c. 1120–30. Stone, $27^1/_2 \times 51''$. Musée Rolin, Autun

The Death of Cain, capital in the cathedral of Saint-Lazare, Autun. Twelfth century

This capital is an excellent example of how Gislebertus, who did the sculpture at Autun, achieved dramatic force with a great economy of means. Cain is struck down by the arrow of Lamech, whose hand is guided by his son Tubalcain.

The Temptation of Christ, ▶ capital in the nave of the church of the Augustins, Plaimpied (Cher). Mid-twelfth century

The artist here rendered the intensity of the spiritual drama by an extreme gesture. His way of depicting the human form resembles that of the capitals in Nazareth (see page 17).

Christ in Glory, tympanum of the church of Perrecy-les-Forges (Saône-et-Loire). c. 1120

The Christ in Glory is sustained by two seraphim whose wings are spread in a most curious manner. These large figures rise above the lintel on which are sculpted scenes of the Passion. Here we recognize the energy and movement which gave such vitality to Burgundian sculpture.

A marvel of Burgundian architecture, Paray-le-Monial shows, on a smaller scale, what the great abbey of ▶ Cluny must once have been like.

Basilica of Paray-le-Monial (Saône-et-Loire). Eleventh–twelfth centuries

◀ *Christ on Horseback at the Center of the Cross, Surrounded by Four Heavenly Knights* (detail). Beginning of twelfth century. Wall painting, total dimensions c. 13′ × 16′ 5″. Crypt of the cathedral of Saint-Étienne, Auxerre (Yonne)

This is the central part of a vast composition which decorates the vault of the crypt.

Count Hugh I of Vaudémont, in Crusader's attire, is embraced by his wife on his return from the Crusades, after nearly sixteen years' absence. The sculpture is in the roughhewn style of the region which is now part of eastern France.

Homecoming of the Crusader, sculptured group from the priory of Belval (Vosges). Third quarter of twelfth century. Church of the Cordeliers, Nancy

Porch of the cathedral of Saint-Trophime, Arles (Bouches-du-Rhône). Last quarter of twelfth century

Last great work of the Provençal Romanesque, the sculpture of the porch in Arles reveals the influence of Roman Antiquity. This can be seen in the friezes, which recall those on sarcophaguses, as well as in the large figures framed by columns. Evident also are connections with the Romanesque art of northern Italy.

Sculpture in the cloister of the cathedral of Saint-Trophime, Arles. End of twelfth century

In southern France, sculpture was rather late in flowering, but its influence on the Gothic sculpture which followed it is undeniable. In these cloisters can be seen, between two Evangelists carved on the corners of a pillar, the stoning of Saint Stephen, which is presented as an action full of dramatic intensity. The medallion which frames a blessing Christ is another proof of the influence of Antiquity, as are also the friezes using the acanthus-leaf pattern.

The Taking of Christ in the Garden of Gethsemane, low relief on the porch of the church of Saint-Gilles-du-Gard (Gard). Second half of twelfth century

Porch of the church of Saint-Gilles-du-Gard (detail). Twelfth century ▶

Provençal Romanesque art produced its masterpiece at Saint-Gilles-du-Gard, where the sculpture reveals more imagination and, at the same time, more refinement than that of the cathedral at Arles. Scenes from the Bible are narrated in a very vigorous manner in low reliefs which run across the width of the façade, rather than on capitals as elsewhere. In the portal (facing page), a distant echo of classical Roman triumphal arches is apparent.

◀ *Martyrdom of Saint Vincent.* Beginning of twelfth century. Wall painting. Former priory of Berzé-la-Ville (Saône-et-Loire)

Christ Blessing, central motif on the front of the altar, church of Saint-Vincent, Avenas (Rhône). c. 1166

There still survive a few Romanesque altars, some in the form of simple altar slabs, others carved in low relief like this one, which is decorated on three sides. The artist appears to have taken his idea from a Carolingian altar frontal in metal. The church itself was founded in 1166 by Louis VII, King of France.

◀ The paintings that embellish the small church of the Cluniac priory of Berzé-la-Ville reveal the obvious influence of the art of the Christian Middle East. Both style and iconography are Byzantine, and this can be explained by the uninterrupted contacts that Cluny had with the Italian abbeys. The exact date of these paintings is still a matter for debate.

Bell tower, cathedral of Saint-Théodorit, Uzès (Gard). Twelfth century

This round bell tower has six stories pierced by double-arched openings and separated by a sawtooth-patterned stringcourse. It is all that remains of the Romanesque cathedral and has certain similarities to the campaniles of Italian churches.

As in many churches in the west of France, this apse is richly decorated with blind arches, engaged columns, moldings, cornices resting on sculptured corbels, and even with small low reliefs with human figures.

Apse, church of Saint-Pierre, Chauvigny (Vienne). Eleventh–twelfth centuries

General view of the monastic buildings, abbey of Thoronet (Var). End of twelfth century

Founded in 1160, the abbey of Thoronet is one of the few great Benedictine abbeys of Provence to come down to us with its general arrangement intact. A simple and austere architecture, devoid of sculptured decoration, it is, nevertheless, not lacking in grandeur.

Abbey of Montmajour (Bouches-du-Rhône). Tenth–fourteenth centuries ▶

Another great monastic construction of Provence, which today is partly in ruins, is the abbey of Montmajour. Its pride is its cloister, one of the finest of Romanesque times. The entire ensemble is dominated by a fortified tower built in the fourteenth century.

The Heavenly Jerusalem. c. 1170. Wall painting. Church of Saint-Chef (Isère)

A high chapel in the gallery of an arm of the transept in what was once the abbey church of Saint-Chef is completely covered with paintings on the rather unusual theme of the Court of Heaven. In the western compartment of the vault, the Heavenly City is symbolized by a building crowned with the Mystic Lamb. Though still strongly influenced by manuscript miniatures, this monumental work—the most extensive that has been preserved in the Dauphiné—has certain stylistic connections with the art of northern Italy.

It is generally thought that these miniatures were done by a monastic workshop in the south of France. Though the drawing and color may lack in delicacy, these paintings are remarkable for their narrative vigor and sense of animation.

Episodes from the History of the Maccabees, in the so-called Atlantic Bible of Florence. Eleventh century. Miniature on parchment, full page $22^1/_2 \times 15^3/_4$″. Ms. Laur. Edili. 126, fol. 99 r., Biblioteca Laurenziana, Florence

◀ Façade, church of Notre-Dame-la-Grande, Poitiers (Vienne). Mid-twelfth century

Nave, church of Saint-Hilaire-le-Grand, Poitiers. Begun 1025, dedicated 1049, rebuilt 1130–68

Saint-Hilaire is one of the most remarkable churches in the west of France on account of the octagonal cupolas built in the twelfth century to cover over the nave which, in the eleventh century, had been roofed only with timberwork.

◀ On the facing page is the best example, and the most elaborate, of Romanesque façades in western France. It is almost entirely covered by monumental sculpture which, however, is also an integral part of the architecture. The façade itself is broad and is balanced harmoniously by two small round towers. For the subject matter of the sculpture, both the Old and the New Testaments were drawn on.

Like the façades, the apses of churches in western France were often richly decorated with sculpture covering almost the entire surface. Such sculpture may be merely decorative, as at Rioux, where a very varied repertory of chiefly geometrical ornament is used. It combines perfectly with its architectural setting, which is made up of blind arcades and arches, and the masonry work itself contributes to the richness of this decoration.

Apse, church of Rioux (Charente-Maritime). Twelfth century

Western France still has some examples of a curious type of funeral monument, of which the Lantern of the Dead at Fenioux is the most complete. It is made up of a cluster of columns terminating in a little circular gallery which is crowned by a pyramid. At night, a light was lit in the gallery of such lanterns set up in the middle of cemeteries.

Lantern of the Dead in the cemetery at Fenioux (Charente-Maritime). Twelfth century

The Weighing of Souls, capital in the church of Saint-Pierre, Chauvigny. First half of twelfth century. Painted stone

Though generally used on tympanums, the various episodes of the Last Judgment are also found on capitals. Here, for example, Saint Michael is seen weighing souls while a demon tries to tilt the balance of the scales. Romanesque sculpture was always painted, and this capital has been restored to reproduce its original, authentic appearance.

Portal and detail of the arch, church of Sainte-Marie-des-Dames, Saintes (Charente-Maritime). Mid-twelfth century ▶

On façades in the regions of Aunis and Saintonge, figurative and decorative sculpture fills the whole of the concentric moldings of the arches above the portals.

The Condemnation and Martyrdom of Saint Savinus. c. 1100. Wall painting. Crypt of the church of Saint-Savin-sur-Gartempe (Vienne)

Scenes from the life of the church's patron saint are depicted in the crypt of Saint-Savin. His martyrdom is shown in several episodes. At the left, he is seen disputing with the Roman governor; at the right, naked, he is put to death in savage fashion. These scenes are painted in a very lively manner, and, in attempting to create an impression of both movement and depth, the artist has introduced architectural settings into his compositions; but these are crudely drawn.

Nave, church of Saint-Savin-sur-Gartempe. Begun 1060, extended 1075–85, then demolished and rebuilt 1095–1115 ▶

Along the whole length of the nave at Saint-Savin, great arches springing from high columns reach up almost to the long continuous barrel vault of the ceiling. The vault is entirely covered with paintings which are arranged in series of rectangular compartments separated by painted bands, and those paintings—a veritable compendium of Biblical stories—have made Saint-Savin world-famous. Even the high columns themselves are painted to simulate marble. The same type of narrative painting is found in the crypt, but with much more subtle drawing and more diversified colors.

Ruins of the abbey church of Notre-Dame, Jumièges (Seine-Inférieure). c. 1040–67

Of the abbey church at Jumièges there remain only the extensive ruins of what was once one of the major Romanesque edifices of Normandy, a region whose influence reached into England and throughout western Europe. An imposing tower rose above the crossing of the transept, and there were galleries around three sides of the crossing. The supports of the nave were made up of an alternation of columns and compound piers.

Apse of the Benedictine abbey church, ▶
Beaulieu. Twelfth century

Here is a good example of how Romanesque apses were built up harmoniously out of a succession of radiating chapels, ambulatory, choir apse, and crossing tower over the transept. The tower is two-storied, with each story constructed on a different plane, and is flanked by stair turrets.

Mistakenly known as "Queen Matilda's Tapestry," this work was done in 1077, probably by English embroiderers at the orders of Odo, Bishop of Bayeux and half brother of the new king, William of Normandy. The conquest of England in 1066 is related in brief scenes which might be said to be the remote ancestors of present-day comic strips.

William the Conqueror Crossing the Channel, detail of the *Bayeux Tapestry*. 1077. Wool embroidery on linen, over-all dimensions 1′ 7$\frac{1}{2}$″ × 229′ 8″. Musée de la Reine Mathilde, Bayeux (Calvados)

The feet of the cross (below) are effigies of the four Evangelists. The various subjects depicted on the base and stem have as their common bond the theme of the Crucifixion and Atonement. It seems that the work itself may be a small version of the great cross which was once in the abbey of Saint-Denis, known now only by the description of it written by Abbot Suger. This piece comes from the abbey of Saint-Bertin in Saint-Omer, and may have been commissioned by Abbot Simon (1177–96) from one of the workshops in the Meuse Valley which specialized in such remarkable, finely executed goldsmith's work.

According to tradition, Empress Matilda, who in a second marriage had become the consort of Geoffrey ▶ Plantagenet, gave this reliquary cross to the abbey of Valasse, which she had founded and where she was to die.

Foot of a cross. 1170–80. Copper with champlevé enamels, $12^1/_4 \times 8^5/_8$″. Museum, Saint-Omer (Somme)

Reliquary of the True Cross from the abbey of Valasse. Third quarter of twelfth century. Gold and gilded silver with filigree work, gems, colored glass, and pearls, $16^{7}/_{8} \times 13''$. Musée des Antiquités, Rouen (Seine-Inférieure)

The so-called Tower of Caesar, Provins (Seine-et-Marne). Before 1137 ▶

The fortified tower at Provins is of a more evolved and better articulated type than that of Falaise. It is made up of a massive central tower on an octagonal plan, with round towers at each of the four corners. This is one of the rare strongholds that have neither been demolished nor suffered from overrestoration.

Falaise is a well-preserved example of the stone constructions which were built on a rectangular ground plan in massive proportions and divided into stories by simple planking. This type of keep appeared in the Loire region as early as the eleventh century and was subsequently taken up in the North.

Donjon of the castle of Falaise (Calvados). Twelfth century

Detail of the façade, church of Azay-le-Rideau (Indre-et-Loire). Beginning of eleventh century

Here is a truly rare example of Romanesque sculpture, one of the first façades to be decorated with stone carvings. The low-relief figures standing under arches represent Christ and the Apostles. Their very rudimentary style suggests a date around the beginning of the eleventh century. Notice the variegated treatment of the masonry on the façade, which adds to the decorative effect. However, what we see here is not the original arrangement of the façade, which was modified later when the window was added.

According to legend, after the destruction of Monte Cassino, the body of Saint Benedict was brought to this abbey, which then became a very much frequented pilgrimage center. The powerfully articulated belfry porch, built over a narthex, is one of the rare examples on such a scale in France where this type of construction, rather like that of the massive west fronts of German churches, was not much favored. The porch contains numerous historiated capitals, which were of great importance in the development of Romanesque sculpture.

Belfry porch, abbey church of Saint-Benoît-sur-Loire (Loiret). End of eleventh century

Nave of the abbey church of Saint-Philibert, Tournus (Saône-et-Loire). First consecration 1019, second consecration 1120

At Tournus there developed the great style of architecture that was to spread to Cluny and the other Burgundian abbeys. Constructed at several different times, the church is notable for the complexity of its interior articulation, the boldness of its elevation, its unusual use of transverse barrel vaults to roof over the nave, and the impression it gives of strength without heaviness, which gives to the whole interior a grandiose aspect.

Crucifixion, stained-glass window in the abbey church of Saint-Remi, Reims (Marne). End of twelfth century

The art of stained glass as practiced in Romanesque times appears here in all of its vigor: boldly constructed figures, a rather restrained palette (here dominated by reds and blues), but with fine effects of spatial depth. Nor is symbolism absent, as can be seen by the chalice placed under the feet of the crucified Christ.

◀ Coronation chalice, known as the Chalice of Saint Remigius. End of twelfth century (cup remade in nineteenth century). Gold, cloisonné and translucent enamels, filigree, precious stones, and pearls, height $6^3/_4''$, diameter $5^7/_8''$. Treasury, Reims Cathedral

LATE ROMANESQUE AND EARLY GOTHIC ART IN FRANCE

Façade, abbey church of Saint-Étienne, Caen (Calvados), known as the Abbaye-aux-Hommes. Façade c. 1060–80, towers thirteenth century

The Romanesque architecture of Normandy is noted for its creative imagination. This explains why it had so much effect on the beginnings of the Gothic style in architecture. In the great abbeys of Caen, with the encouragement of the Dukes of Normandy who had become Kings of England, the first experiments in vaulting were undertaken, and there too was perfected the type of façade with double towers. In the thirteenth century, the two towers of Saint-Étienne were capped with superb Gothic spires which are in complete harmony with them.

Nave, cathedral of Notre-Dame, Bayeux. c. 1150 ▶

Norman architecture is distinguished not only for its fruitful experiments but also for an original vocabulary of decorative motifs, as exemplified in the nave of the cathedral at Bayeux, where the numerous geometrical motifs seem almost to be a survival of the so-called "barbarian" art of the pre-Romanesque era. The diagonally ribbed vault was a later addition.

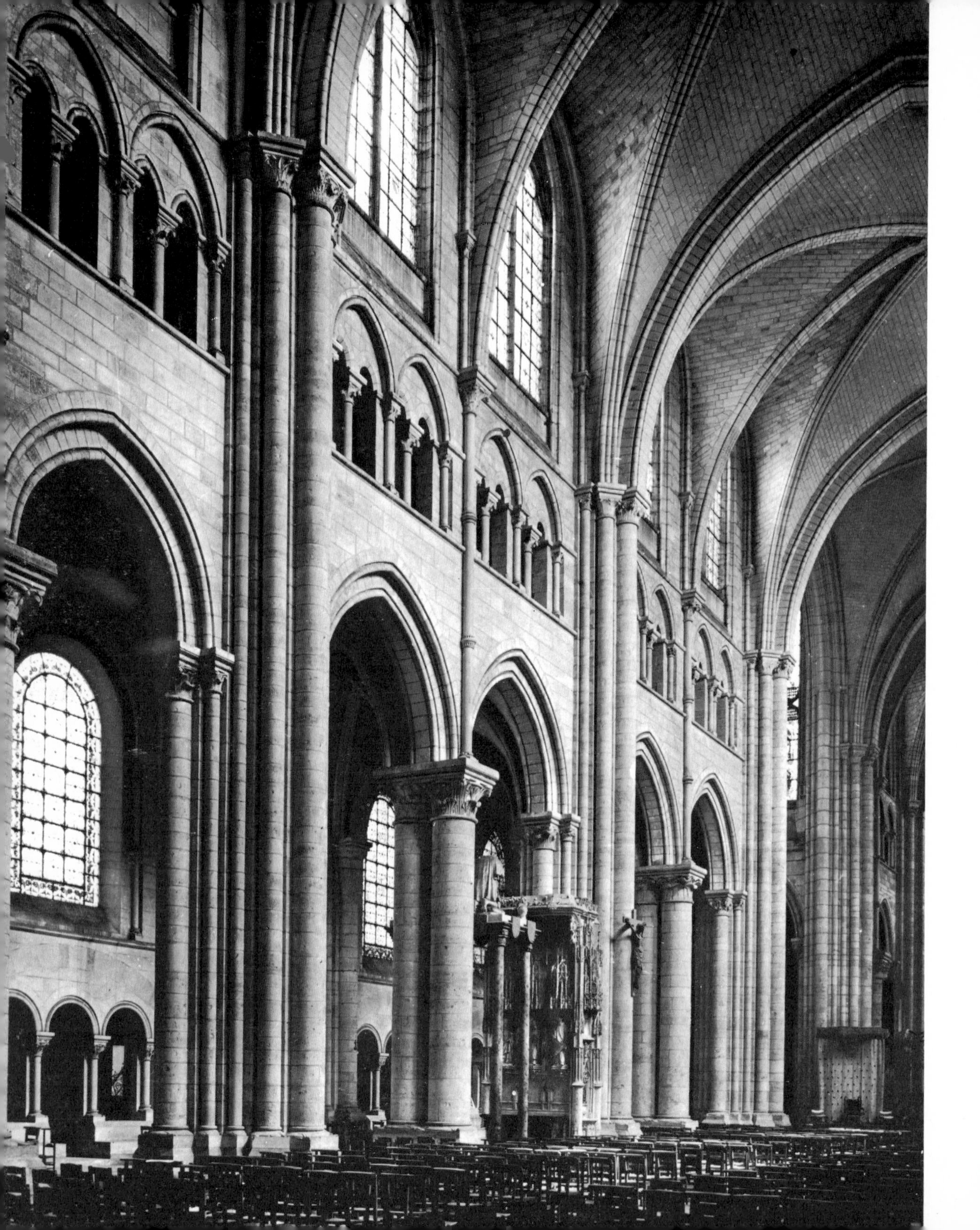

◀ View of the nave, cathedral of Sens (Yonne). First section of nave consecrated in 1164

The cathedral at Sens can be said to be the first great Gothic cathedral, and its influence was considerable both on the Continent and in England. The emphasis on height, the stress placed on articulations which are accented by small columns and moldings, the sexpartite vaulting done with diagonal ribs and involving an alternation of the supports (compound piers and double columns)—all these elements belong to the new style, but they are treated here in a spirit which brings to mind the great Romanesque sanctuaries.

Façade, cathedral of Laon (Aisne). End of twelfth and beginning of thirteenth centuries

Almost contemporary with Notre-Dame in Paris, Notre-Dame of Laon is the most perfect example of a cathedral built at the dawn of the Gothic age, though it still remains very close to Romanesque architecture in its basic structure (the interior elevation, the position of the towers). The west façade with its great rose window, its towers with their multiple projections, its very deep portals, all nevertheless constitute an original conception which is earlier in date than that of the cathedral of Paris. What we have here is, in fact, the first great Gothic façade incorporating twin towers.

Adoration of the Magi. Mid-twelfth century. Stone relief.
Church of Sainte-Croix, La Charité-sur-Loire (Nièvre)

La Charité-sur-Loire, affiliated with the order of Cluny, was an important halting place on the great pilgrimage route. It still contains extensive fragments of the sculpture that once decorated the church. This relief is evidence of the vigorous art being done at the time of transition from the Romanesque to the new Gothic style. It is not unrelated to the sculpture on the Royal Portal at Chartres, whose significance in the genesis of Gothic art is universally admitted.

◀ Vase in the form of an eagle. c. 1140. Antique porphyry and silver gilt, height 16 7/8″. The Louvre, Paris

This is one of the most curious and most precious of the treasures that once belonged to the abbey of Saint-Denis. The famous Abbot Suger, who presented it to his abbey, was responsible for its astonishing transformation from an Antique vase into an eagle.

Head from the tomb effigy of King Lothair. Mid-twelfth century. Painted stone, height 11″. Musée Lapidaire, Reims

◄ The sculptured head, opposite, belonged to the statue on the tomb of the Carolingian King Lothair, who was buried in 986 in the choir of Saint-Remi at Reims. However, the tomb effigy was not made until long after his death, around the middle of the twelfth century. The tomb was broken up in the French Revolution, and the head was rediscovered only when excavations were carried out in 1919. The head is encircled by a crown with four *fleurons*, beneath which the hair ends, as does the beard, in stylized curls all of the same form and size. The delicate workmanship points to an evolution toward the early Gothic style of northern France. There are still traces of the color used to heighten the features.

Head of Christ, detail of crucifix in the collegiate church of Saint-Laurent, Auzon (Haute-Loire). Twelfth century. Wood, total height $74^3/_4''$

The sensitive modeling of the face confirms that, in the second half of the twelfth century, art was striving toward the presentation of a more human expression. At the dawn of the Gothic, the artist made of the crucified Christ a suffering and piteous being, at the same time retaining something of Romanesque linearity, as shown by the way the hair and beard are rendered by parallel grooves. Other examples of such Late Romanesque Christs are found in this region, where the collegiate church of Auzon was a dependency of the abbey of La Chaise-Dieu. They are all represented with open eyes and wearing a colobium, a short-sleeved tunic. It was above all in the Auvergne region that such sculpture in the round developed.

Christ Blessing, Surrounded by the Symbols of the Evangelists, tympanum of the Royal Portal, Chartres Cathedral (Eure-et-Loir). 1145–55

Here is a truly calm and noble art, evidence of the achievements of the new Gothic style. It is more spacious in composition, more varied in postures, and has a greater awareness of human traits, though as yet it is still far from naturalistic.

Entry of Christ into Jerusalem, stained-glass window from the west façade, Chartres Cathedral. c. 1150

In Gothic churches, the walls were opened up to permit light to pass through and, in so doing, to create a mystical atmosphere by the use of stained glass, which was to become one of the most notable manifestations of Gothic art. From the beginning, as we see here, an astonishing richness of composition and color was achieved in stained-glass windows. The palms and personages in the background weave an arabesque around the principal figure of the Christ who, in completely convincing manner, sits astride an entirely credible animal.

Façade and west tower, Ely Cathedral (Cambridgeshire). 1083–late twelfth century

ROMANESQUE ART IN ENGLAND

It was in 1083, a few years after William of Normandy conquered England, that work was begun on the vast minster which was elevated to the dignity of cathedral while it was still being built. Ely Cathedral reflects almost every stage of English Romanesque style and also comprises important Gothic additions, such as the porch and the top story of the imposing tower. The west part represents the final phase of the Romanesque, the last quarter of the twelfth century, with a rich articulation of forms which lead imperceptibly to the Gothic. Ely, in fact, does give the impression of unity, despite all the different phases of its construction, for it seems that the grandiose plan initially laid down by the Norman Abbot Simeon was always kept in mind. Some 535 feet in length, Ely has two transepts, one in the eastern part, one in the western, and it is obvious that its builders had profited by the lessons of Norman architecture.

Nave, Ely Cathedral. c. 1090–1180 ▶

The influence of some model in Normandy itself is to be seen in the powerful ternary rhythm of this immense nave with double moldings on the pier arches, its gallery opened up by twinned bays under relieving arches, and its clerestory windows behind a gallery passageway. Particularly noteworthy is the sobriety of the architecture, which makes no appeal through sculptural decoration but draws its grandeur only from the harmony of its mass and line. The nave is covered by a wooden ceiling and has no less than twelve bays with cylindrical piers alternating with piers composed of clusters of small columns.

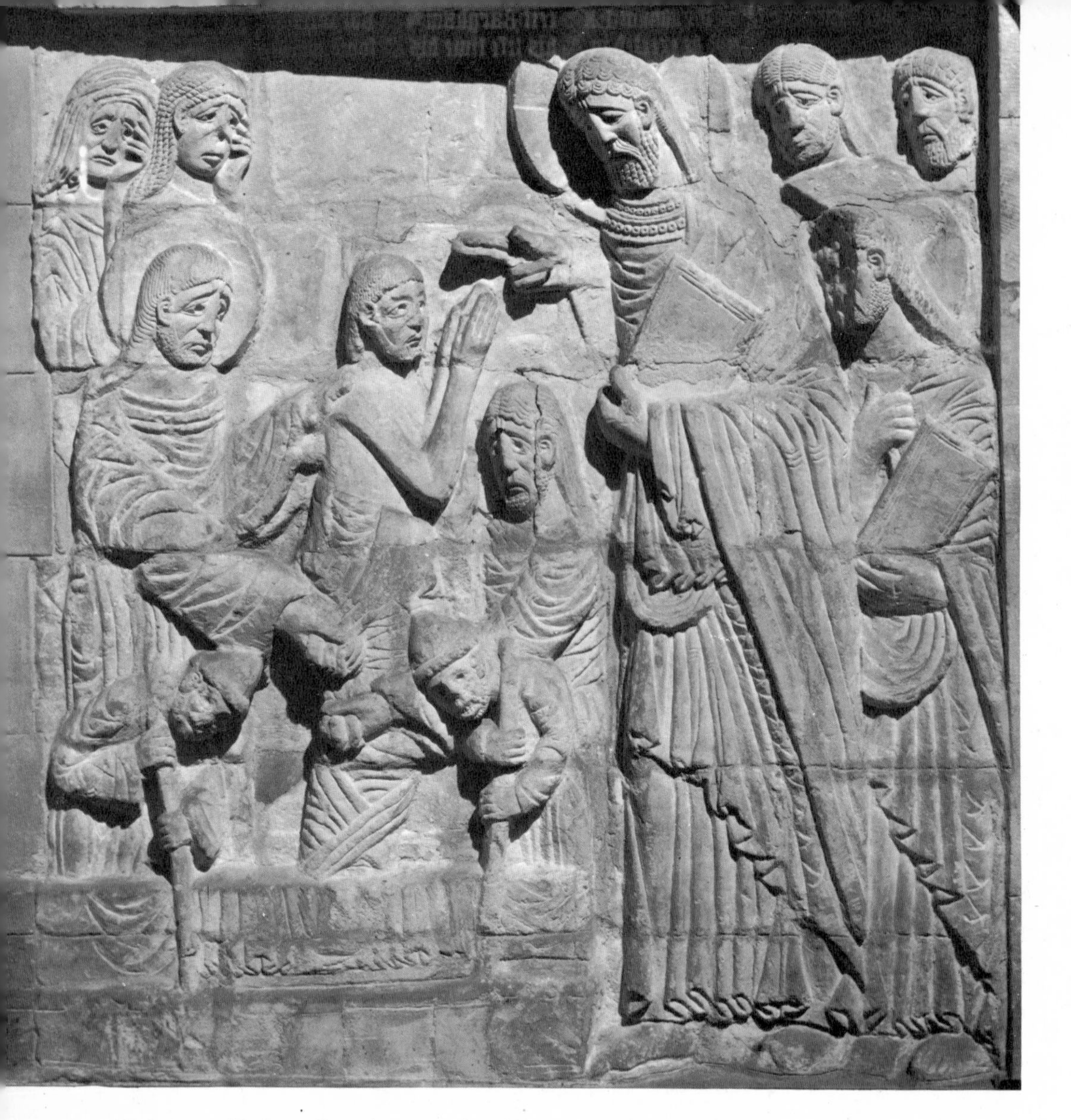

The Raising of Lazarus. Second quarter of twelfth century (?). Stone relief, height c. 44″. South aisle of the choir, Chichester Cathedral (Sussex)

These Chichester reliefs have no equal elsewhere in England, where such a vast quantity of church sculpture was destroyed in the sixteenth century, and it may be that they were done by a sculptor from the Continent.

Nave, Durham Cathedral. 1093–1133 ▶

Begun in 1093 by Bishop William of Calais, this abbey church (which, like Ely, also became a cathedral) was constructed in forty years. It represents an important landmark in the history of architecture, because its builders, who here too were Normans, conceived it to carry an ogival vault, a form destined to rise to great favor and, in a sense, to give birth to the Gothic style.

The Creation of Eve, from the Bible of Saint Castor's. 1067–77. Miniature on parchment, $17^3/_4 \times 13^1/_4$″. Staatsbibliothek, Bamberg (Bavaria) ▶

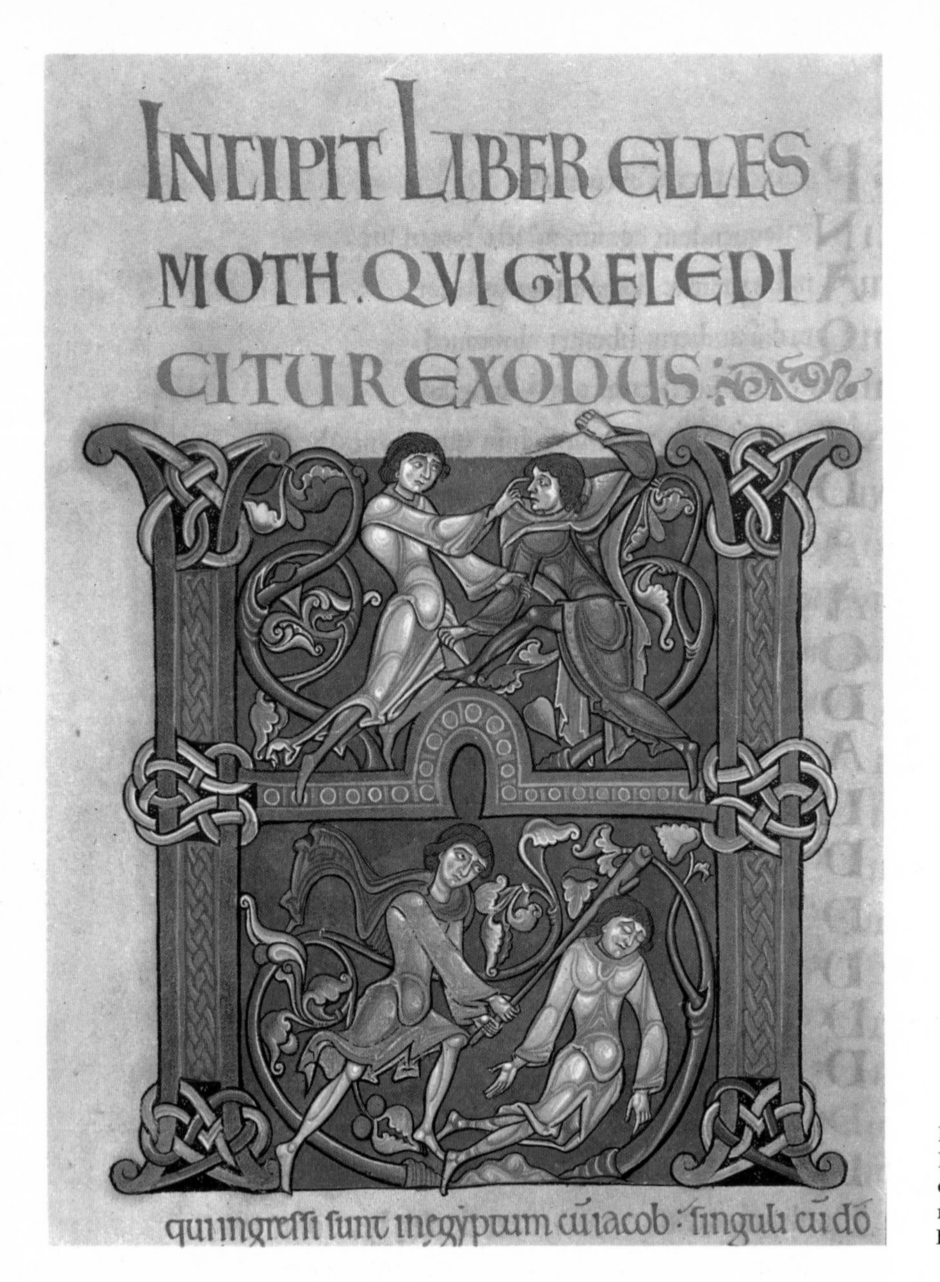

Initial letter of the Book of Exodus, in the so-called Winchester Bible. c. 1160. Illumination on parchment. Cathedral Library, Winchester (Hampshire)

With remarkable virtuosity, the miniaturist multiplied his arabesques and knotwork, twining them between and around the human figures. Above, there is an Egyptian slaying a Hebrew, and below this we see the vengeance of Moses. Here we find the subtle and refined art of the English monastic scribes as practiced at Winchester, a center of civilization from early times which did not forget the traditions of Irish ornamental art.

Noteworthy in the miniature on the facing page is the attempt to create a landscape merely by sketching in two different kinds of trees as a frame for the composition. ▶

Coniugit ex costa per xpm condit eua · Et dat ei sponsam · quia femine post mala uiadam :
Suasit ei uentrum mulierc ula tumere malo · Per qd gustauit n felix pocula leti :

Candlestick from the monastery of Gloucester. c. 1110. Gilt bell metal, height 23″. Victoria & Albert Museum, London

This candlestick, which was given to his monastery by the Abbot Peter (1104–13), is one of the finest preserved from that period. The subject depicted is the struggle between Good and Evil, as shown by the tangle of bodies of men and animals within the scrollwork. The way they are twined and twisted together recalls certain monumental *trumeaux*, such as that at Souillac, and is found also in miniatures of the time. The work was executed by an Anglo-Norman workshop.

ROMANESQUE ART IN THE LOW COUNTRIES

Swearing of an Oath before an Emperor. Beginning of thirteenth century. ▶
High relief in stone. Onze Lieve Vrouwekerk, Maastricht (Holland)

The sculptured scene shows the ceremony in which an oath is taken before the Emperor and is sworn on the *cappa* of Saint Martin. Certain churches were endowed with the privilege of *cappella*, and this dignity was awarded to the church at Maastricht in 1204, which enables us to assign an approximate date to this relief. Behind the Emperor seated on his throne, an attendant brings the Imperial sword, while the candidate for the oath kneels before the sovereign. The work is still completely Romanesque, as much in spirit as in composition and style. Only the effort to lend more animation to the scene and to introduce realistic details gives some sense of progress.

West front, Onze Lieve Vrouwekerk, Maastricht. Eleventh–twelfth centuries

The Church of Our Lady in Maastricht has a west choir opening onto the nave. Its exterior resembles a veritable fortress. The immense wall of the façade, framed by two round stair turrets, is almost blank, with only a few windows and no portal. Perhaps no other west front of the type so frequent in the Imperial cities more fully sums up just what is meant by the "Imperial style."

North façade of the nave and transept, cathedral of Notre-Dame, Tournai (Belgium). Eleventh–twelfth centuries ▶

The great church of Tournai, on the border between Germanic- and French-speaking regions, took something of its architectural style from both those worlds. The nave has an imposing elevation, four stories high. The austere exterior, decorated by series of arcades, is especially notable for the five towers which thrust upward above the transept, the lantern tower being surrounded by the towers over each of the four arms of the crossing. Each of those arms ends in a semicircular apse. The rise of the Gothic style in northern France owed much to this cathedral.

This is the earliest example of the goldsmith's art in the Meuse Valley which can be dated with precision: it was on April 13, 1145, that the holy relics were placed in this reliquary. The head has all the majesty of Roman busts of the Late Empire, while Byzantine influence and recollections of "barbarian" art mingle on the base without clashing. On the base, the half-length figures of Pope Alexander and his disciples on plaques of champlevé enamel are separated from each other by broad bands studded with cabochons. This particularly venerable work can be attributed with some probability to the goldsmith Godefroy of Huy, since he was acquainted with Wibald, the abbot of Stavelot, who gave this bust to his monastery.

GODEFROY OF HUY, attributed. Reliquary head of Saint Alexander the Pope. 1145. Head in repoussé silver, engraved and gilded; wooden base covered with champlevé enamels, engraved brass plaques, and plaques studded with beads of crystal and precious stones; feet in cast bronze; height of head 13″, over-all height with base $17^1/_2$″. Musées Royaux d'Art et d'Histoire, Brussels

RENIER OF HUY. Baptismal font. ▶ 1107–18. Cast bronze, height 25″. Church of Saint-Barthélemy, Liège (Belgium)

In the twelfth century, the region of the Meuse witnessed the expansion of its celebrated goldsmiths' workshops, whose products were exported throughout Western Christendom. The supple, noble art of a classical equilibrium which was developed in the Mosan region took up again the traditions of the Carolingian and Ottonian renaissances. The baptismal font executed by Renier of Huy for the abbey of Notre-Dame-aux-Fonts is the most remarkable example of this art. The font, decorated with large low reliefs on subjects connected with baptism, is supported on the backs of small bulls.

Jacob's Ladder and the Erection of an Altar at Bethel. c. 1160. Illumination on parchment, $9^{3}/_{4} \times 6^{1}/_{8}$″. Ms. 78 A 6, fol. 4 v., Kupferstichkabinett, Berlin-Dahlem ▶

This miniature of Mosan origin was not designed to illustrate a text but perhaps was part of a book of models for artists, either painters or sculptors. The figures, with their fluid drawing, show stylistic connections with those on the baptismal font of Renier of Huy (see page 97).

Saint John the Evangelist. Mid-twelfth century. Miniature from a Gospel Book, $12^{5}/_{8} \times 8^{5}/_{8}$″. Hessische Landes- und Hochschulbibliothek, Darmstadt

This miniature with its gold background and very elegant drawing, especially notable in the drapery, comes from a great monastic center in Flanders, perhaps Saint-Omer, or from the Mosan area, possibly from Liège itself.

fugiente iacob aram ex precepto matris. dormiens in quodam loco. vidit in sompnis scalam stantem super terram,
cacumen et tangens celum. angelos quoque dei ascendentes et descendentes per eam. dominumque innixum scale

iacob

bethel

evigilans iacob de [illegible] ait vere deus est in loco isto [illegible] nesciebam [illegible] pavensque [illegible] locus iste [illegible]
Surgensque [illegible] lapidem [illegible] quem supposuerat capiti suo erexit in titulum. fundens [illegible] desuper.

ROMANESQUE ART IN GERMANY

Ruins of the Benedictine abbey church of Limburg an der Haardt (Palatinate). 1025–45

The church was founded in 1025 by Emperor Conrad II and consecrated in 1042. The view shown here is of the north arm of the crossing with, at the right, the chancel arch, which was walled up in the sixteenth century. The Imperial character of the construction is emphasized by the great arches which give rhythm to the elevation. A wooden ceiling once covered the edifice just above the clerestory windows.

Nave, cathedral of Sankt-Maria-und-Stephan, Speyer (Palatinate). Eleventh–twelfth centuries, largely restored and remodeled in eighteenth, nineteenth, and twentieth centuries (frescoes done 1846–53) ▶

The impressive elevation of the nave of the Imperial cathedral of Speyer is the product of two separate stages of work. The responds with their engaged half columns, which support the transverse ribs of the vault, and the arches framing the windows were added around 1100. The strong rhythm of the double bays produces an impression of upward thrust and of nobility, even though there is no decoration other than that of the architectonic elements themselves.

The great Romanesque cathedrals of the Germanic realm almost always contained a large crypt built under the choir. These crypts were composed of three aisles separated by supporting columns. That of the Imperial cathedral of Speyer is one of the most immense and imposing of such crypts, which are, in fact, virtually churches beneath churches.

Crypt of the cathedral of Speyer. Consecrated in 1041

Abbey church of Maria Laach (near Coblenz, Rhineland). Cornerstone laid c. 1093, cloister completed 1127, the "Paradise Garden" atrium 1220–30

The church of the Benedictine abbey of Maria Laach, with its rich variety of towers, is one of the most refined constructions of the Romanesque art of the Rhineland. The west front was built a little later than the nave and the choir, and is extended in front by a sort of forecourt or atrium resembling a three-sided cloister. This is the so-called "Paradise Garden," which was not built until the beginning of the thirteenth century.

The Rhenish style was always quite varied in its plans as well as in its interior and exterior articulation. The style extended into the Vosges area, as can be seen at Saint-Dié, where the piers have the same sort of alternation of strong and weak accents, the weak ones marked by half columns which are curiously interrupted at the level of the cornice. The nave and aisles are covered by groined vaults.

Nave, church of Notre-Dame, Saint-Dié (Vosges). Twelfth century

Also in the Vosges is the ▶ abbey church of Murbach, of which only the eastern section remains as impressive evidence of the severity and majesty of the Imperial style of the Rhineland.

Abbey church of Murbach (Haut-Rhin). First half of twelfth century

Portal of Saint Gall, cathedral of Basel (Switzerland). 1170–1200

The old cathedral in Basel, dating from the beginning of the eleventh century, was replaced at the end of the twelfth century by a new edifice in which the new influences mingled with those of the Ottonian tradition. The Saint Gall portal, which quite early was moved from the west façade to that of the north arm of the transept, was the first important portal in Imperial territory to be decorated with sculpture. Sin and the Last Judgment are the themes, with Christ the Judge on the tympanum and the Wise and Foolish Virgins on the lintel. Statues of Apostles are set between the columns which support the arches. On small projections under the cornice are little low reliefs illustrating the theme of Sin, and in two niches framing the archivolt angels sound trumpets. These sculptures are far from uniform in style, and this is true also of the over-all arrangement of the portal. This is understandable, because Basel was at the confluence of the stylistic currents of the West and those of the Rhineland.

The striving after grandeur and majesty typical of Imperial Germanic art relives in this hallucinating figure in which the Emperor proclaims himself Vicar of God and, at the same time, successor of the ancient Caesars. The stained-glass window, with its uncompromising design, doubtless came from the former west front of the cathedral which preceded the new Imperial edifice built by Frederick Barbarossa.

An Emperor, stained-glass window from the former Romanesque cathedral of Strasbourg (Bas-Rhin). c. 1200. Cathedral Museum, Strasbourg

Lectern from the monastery of Alpirsbach. c. 1150. Wood with original paintwork. City church, Freudenstadt (Württemberg)

This is an example of the artistic activity which developed in the monastic centers affiliated to the congregation of Hirsau. The lectern has the four Evangelists carved in the round and carrying on their shoulders a reading desk decorated with the four symbols of the Evangelists cut in low relief. The draperies of the figures cling tightly to the bodies, and the entire work is carved from one piece of limewood, which imposed certain limitations on the artist. The Evangelists with their elongated faces, ascetic features, and meditative mien testify to the mystical austerity of the Benedictine reform which took place at Hirsau. Of special note is the varied treatment of the hair of each figure.

Detail of the lectern on the facing page

Church of the Apostles, Cologne. Begun early eleventh century, apse built after 1192

West front, cathedral of Trier (Rhineland). 1016–47

This is one of the most harmonious achievements to result from the experiments of the Rhenish architects: a triapsidal choir imitating that of Sankt Maria im Kapitol in Cologne, arcaded galleries crowning the apses, and towers of a variety of designs, heights, and sizes.

It was at the cathedral in Trier that the inventive genius of the Imperial architects reached its apogee. They introduced an infinite variety in effects of mass and volume, in contrasts between solid surfaces and hollows, and all of this in a carefully studied articulation designed to exalt the grandeur of the Imperial principle. Above all, the west front was conceived as an expression of that principle, as shown by the deliberate imitation of great Roman buildings of which many still survived in Trier. The lesson of Trier was taken up elsewhere in the Germanic regions, as can be seen in Cologne.

Mainz was the last of the great Imperial cathedrals of the Rhineland. Its western part, with the transept and the triapsidal choir, displays the final exuberant flowering of German Romanesque art at a time when France was already building its great Gothic cathedrals. ▶

Civil edifices of the Romanesque period are rare in Germany. Where they exist, more often than not they are grossly altered, as at Wimpfen, or in ruins, as is the case with what was once the palace of Frederick Barbarossa at Gelnhausen. These impressive ruins still show clearly all the care that was lavished on the construction of the Imperial residences. Noteworthy is the effort made to use the light to the fullest in the interiors, in this case by a series of arcaded window openings, which reveal not only a desire for comfort but also for much greater magnificence than would have been necessary if this were meant only to be a fortified castle. This is, indeed, more of a palace than a fortress.

Ruins of the Imperial Palace at Gelnhausen (Hesse).
Begun under Emperor Frederick Barbarossa (1152–90)

West apse, cathedral of Sankt-Martin-und-Stephan, Mainz (Rhenish-Hesse). 1009–1243 (the tall western crossing tower added by F. I. M. Neumann in 1769–74)

Crossing, church of Sankt Georg, Limburg a. d. Lahn ▶

Church of Sankt Georg, Limburg an der Lahn (Hesse). First half of thirteenth century

Raised up on a rock overhanging the river, the old collegiate church of Limburg proudly flaunts its seven towers. The exterior is richly decorated with arcades, while the interior, with its four-storied elevation, its ample galleries that encircle the building, its arcaded triforium, and its sexpartite vaults on their alternately strong and weak supports, betrays beyond question the influence of the great cathedral of Laon—an influence which extended well into German territory. After a long resistance, Romanesque art was destined to lose ground, but in this church the massiveness of the great arcades on the ground floor shows how the old tradition persisted.

◀ Portal, church of Sankt Jakob, Coesfeld (Westphalia). Mid-thirteenth century

All that remains of the church of Sankt Jakob, which was destroyed in the last war, is this portal, richly decorated with geometrical and stylized floral motifs. East of the Rhine, sculptured decoration was rarely figurative in a Romanesque art which persisted until the middle of the thirteenth century and, in some places, even longer.

Westwork, collegiate church of Sankt Patroklus, Soest (Westphalia). 1200–20

Sankt Patroklus is one of the most important examples of this type of construction. Its open arcade on the ground floor is surmounted by three arched windows, behind which there is a sort of Imperial loggia, and the whole is crowned by the powerful square tower with its four smaller bell turrets. There are reminiscences of the old Roman style, and one senses the desire to affirm the importance of this city as both an Imperial and an ecclesiastical center.

Interior of the Bishop's Chapel, Idensen (Hanover). 1120–40

This tiny building with a single nave and transept was constructed by Sigward, Bishop of Minden from 1120 to 1140, to serve as his own burial place. The groined vaults are separated by transverse arches in a manner which recalls certain Cappadocian sanctuaries built over the tombs of martyrs. Oriental influence appears also in the Byzantinesque paintings which cover all the interior walls with scenes from the Old Testament and from the life of Saint Peter.

All Saints' Chapel, cathedral of Sankt Peter, Regensburg (Bavaria). c. 1160

Here, the bishop had this chapel built against the cloisters of the cathedral as his funerary chapel. The circular plan, with its careful geometrical proportions, makes one think, here too, of inspiration from Asia Minor; and in fact it is known that certain German bishops did send emissaries to the East to make measurements and sketches of ancient Christian edifices.

North portal and a detail of the sculptured decoration (facing page), façade of the Schottenkirche Sankt Jakob, Regensburg. Early twelfth century

Constructed by Irish monks established in Regensburg (known always as Scots, hence "Schottenkirche"), the portal with its sculptured decoration is somewhat disconcerting in effect, not only because of its style but also because of its iconography, in which people and fabulous animals are jumbled together on the low reliefs scattered over the wall of the façade.

One of the rare portals of the German Romanesque with figurative sculpture, the forms of the Golden Portal remain Romanesque but the spirit is already Gothic. There are statues not only on the jambs but also on the arches, where they alternate with an elaborate geometrical decoration reminiscent of the Norman Romanesque. On the tympanum is a low relief with the Virgin holding the Christ child on her knees, flanked by the Magi and by angels adoring the Infant. The portal was originally painted, as was always the case with such sculpture in the Middle Ages, and its name comes from the fact that, here, the dominant color was gold.

The Golden Portal, church of Sankt Maria, Freiberg (Saxony). Second quarter of thirteenth century

Cathedral of Sankt Peter, Bamberg. 1203–37

The cathedral of Bamberg was reconstructed at the beginning of the thirteenth century with the same dimensions as the original edifice, which dated from the beginning of the eleventh century. It is a basilica with a double choir and with a transept at the west end, and it possesses all the magnitude of an Imperial cathedral. A pair of tall many-storied, square towers flanks each of the choirs. The west towers, built during the last stage of construction shortly before the consecration in 1237, are particularly interesting. The corners of the towers are ornamented with small colonnaded niches, which no doubt were influenced by similar forms on the cathedral at Laon. Unfortunately the cathedral was excessively restored in the nineteenth century, but it has preserved some of the most remarkable sculpture from the beginning of Gothic times in which French influence can be traced.

Nave, collegiate church of Sankt Servatius, Quedlinburg (Saxony-Anhalt). End of eleventh–beginning of twelfth centuries

Covered with a wooden ceiling, this basilical type of church has large arches which demonstrate a characteristic of this region: the alternation of two columns, a square pier, and then again two columns. At the west end there is a gallery which is, in fact, a reduced massive west front. The capitals of the nave are ornamented by sculpture in which monsters appear in the midst of stylized foliage and geometrical motifs in a style not unrelated to that of Sant'Abbondio at Como in Lombardy (see page 201). The church was consecrated in 1129 and for several centuries sheltered a chapter of noblewomen.

Nave with view of choir and crypt, monastery church of Jerichow (Brandenburg). Second half of twelfth century ▶

The Premonstratensian church in Jerichow is one of the last and most harmonious creations of German Romanesque architecture. Constructed in brick, it has broad semicircular arches, thick cylindrical pillars with trapezoidal capitals, and a raised choir over the crypt—all combining to make an ample, calm, and spacious interior.

ECCE CRVCEM DNI FVGITE PARTES ADVERSE

Reliquary of the Holy Cross, from the abbey of Stavelot (Belgium). Eleventh–twelfth centuries. Engraved copper gilt; stenciled silver gilt; precious stones; enamels with burned varnish ground; champlevé enamels; embossed silver, height 25³/₄″. Pierpont Morgan Library, New York

In 1154, the Abbot Wibald, who had been sent to Constantinople as ambassador for Emperor Frederick Barbarossa, acquired there two small reliquary triptychs containing pieces of the True Cross. On his return to his abbey of Stavelot, he had the reliquaries set into the central panel of a much larger triptych. On the side wings, medallions made of champlevé enamel tell the story of the Invention of the True Cross in highly picturesque scenes which are explained in the accompanying inscriptions.

The Virgin and Child of Imad. Eleventh century. Freestanding wooden statue, height 44″. Erzbischöfliches Diözesanmuseum, Paderborn (Westphalia)

◀ This statue, once covered with gold leaf, was a gift of the Bishop Imad in 1058 to his cathedral. Right at the outset, the Romanesque style produced here a work still marked by Byzantine rigidity but which, through its rigorous treatment of large planes squared off by simple straight furrows, has a certain nobility and an undeniable power of expression.

Virgin and Child. Twelfth century. Stone, height 35$^1/_2$″. Sankt Maria im Kapitol, Cologne

Despite a certain stiffness which recalls the Romanesque, this work is marked by the growing influence of the Gothic style of northern France, especially in its striving after expressiveness. Iconographically the statue is unusual, in that Jesus is presented, not as an infant, but as a grown child. There are still traces of the color with which sculpture was customarily painted at the time.

Crypt (facing page) and a detail of a sculptured pillar, cathedral of Sankt Maria und Korbinian, Freising (Bavaria). Second half of twelfth century. Tufa stone

Because we know that Bishop Eberhard was buried in this crypt in 1164, we have some idea of the date of its construction. Made up of four aisles with nine bays, the vault is supported by three rows of square or cylindrical pillars, several of which have capitals sculptured in relief, some with figures. However, the most important sculpture is that covering an entire pillar on which, in a rough and extravagant style, the artist intermixed people and monstrous animals which attempt to devour the human figures. The theme is frequent in Romanesque art, symbolizing the assault of the forces of Evil upon mankind. The same theme appears on the famous doorpost at Souillac in France where, however, it is treated with much more refinement. Such a bestiary of stylized monsters and rudimentary human figures nevertheless suggests that the German artist was still working within the tradition of "barbarian" art of northern Europe.

Capitals in the church of Sankt Godehard, Hildesheim (Lower Saxony). 1133–72

Low relief in the apse of the parish church of Maria Geburt, Schöngrabern (Lower Austria). Beginning of thirteenth century

Strange low reliefs decorate the semicircular apse of the church at Schöngrabern. The style is highly archaic, if not primitive, but is not without a certain expressive power. It is folk art, perhaps, but at any rate has absolutely no connection with the Gothic style which was in full sway elsewhere. The iconography of the scenes is even more mysterious and, as yet, has not been deciphered. Who is the figure on a throne receiving offerings, with a monstrous bird beneath his feet, lying on its back and in the act of devouring a tiny human being? Can it be that these reliefs were conceived as some sort of magical image intended to conjure away the dark forces of Evil? Attempts have been made to relate the reliefs to those of the Schottenkirche Sankt Jakob in Regensburg (see page 121) or even to those of the church in Suzdal on the Nerl, a tributary of the Volga.

◀ Erected after the canonisation of Bishop Godehard in 1131 and consecrated in 1172, this edifice in pure Romanesque style contains much important sculpture. The capitals are decorated with abstract motifs such as knotwork, palmettos, braids, checkerboards, and dentils. A few, however, have figures designed to fit the cuboid form common to capitals in this region, another characteristic of which is the large abacus projecting above the bell. The style here is still stiff but produces remarkable decorative effects.

The sculptured decoration of the cylindrical font is divided into two tiers by a band bearing an inscription. Above, under the arches spanning capitals capped by turrets, are scenes from the life of Christ. Christ in Glory appears in a mandorla surrounded by the symbols of the Evangelists. Below are monsters symbolic of the forces of Evil crushed by the grace of baptism. The technique, which is refined, is reminiscent of that used on ivories in Asia Minor.

◀ Baptismal font. 1129. Stone. Former monastic church, Freckenhorst (Westphalia)

Baptismal font. c. 1220–30. Bronze, height 71″. Cathedral of Sankt Maria, Hildesheim ▶

Among the treasures of the cathedral of Hildesheim—a major religious center in the Middle Ages—is its baptismal font, a remarkable work in bronze which was produced by the local workshops and, in spite of its late date, was still conceived in the spirit of the Romanesque. The four Rivers of Paradise, three-dimensional figures, kneel to support the basin like four atlantes. The font and its lid are entirely covered with low reliefs of scenes from the life of Christ, which are modeled in a flowing and animated style.

Gilbertus was the first abbot of Maria Laach, and it was he who, from 1112 on, actively encouraged the work of building, insisting that the choir be completed promptly in order to permit the regular functioning of the monastic offices. After his death in 1152, an effigy in mosaic in Byzantine style, accompanied by an inscription, was placed on his tomb in the crypt of the abbey church.

Tomb slab of Abbot Gilbertus, from the abbey of Maria Laach. Second half of twelfth century. Mosaic, $45^1/_4 \times 28^1/_4''$. Rheinisches Landesmuseum, Bonn

Christ in Majesty. Mid-twelfth century. Stone low relief. Church of Sankt Peter, Petersberg, near Fulda (Hesse) ▶

The Christ in Majesty, seated and blessing with one hand while holding a book in the other, is one of the most frequent themes in Romanesque art, and it is interesting to see how it is interpreted in different regions. Here, there is still an underlying Byzantine hieratic rigidity. The coarse grain of the stone and the artist's rather limited knowledge of his craft render the work heavy, with all its contours and volumes thick and, so to speak, doughy.

Crucifix. Last third of eleventh century. Polychromed wood, height 65$^{3}/_{4}$″. Former abbey church, Benninghausen (Westphalia)

This is a replica of the crucifix of Gero in the cathedral of Cologne, a highly venerated work from the end of the tenth century. The replica comes from the last phase of the Ottonian era and the earliest period of Romanesque art. Its stylization is pronounced, as can be seen in the carving of the tendons and ribs, in the parallel folds of the drape, and in the emaciated features of the face. All of these are characteristic of an expressiveness which was carried to its limits in the Ottonian art of this region. In spirit, at least, such emphasis on pathos connects this crucifix with the violence of certain Spanish works.

IMERWARD. Crucifix. End of twelfth century. Wood. Cathedral of Sankt Blasius, Brunswick (Lower Saxony)

This type of Christ, in a long tunic with parallel pleats, is altogether strange: such a manner of sculpture has no connection with any other in the German art of this period. However, such images are not rare in Spain, and the *Volto Santo* of Lucca in Italy, which is dated 1200, resembles this Christ. The statue is signed *Imerward me fecit* (Imerward made me) and the name at least seems to be German. Nevertheless, one wonders if it might not be a work brought back from the Crusades by someone like Henry the Lion, Duke of Brunswick.

Head of Christ, detail of a crucifix. c. 1070. Bronze and silver, height of entire crucifix $39^{1}/_{2}''$. Treasury, cathedral of Sankt Peter und Gorgonius, Minden (Westphalia)

IMERWARD. Head of Christ, detail of the crucifix of Brunswick (see page 139) ▶

The Minden crucifix belongs to the transition period between the Ottonian and Romanesque styles. This head of Christ is one of the masterworks of sculpture of the time, above all because of its deeply moving expression of suffering. The face of the Imerward Christ (facing page) is less human but no less fascinating.

The Annunciation to the Shepherds, detail of the wooden reliefs on the door of Sankt Maria im Kapitol, Cologne. c. 1050 ▶

Descent from the Cross. c. 1115. Stone, height 18′. Externsteine, near Horn (Westphalia)

This gigantic low relief, carved out of a rocky wall, depicts Golgotha with a mixture of realism and symbolism and in a primitive and angular style which is far removed from any possible Byzantine models. The Externsteine rocks were the object of Christian pilgrimages after having been a place of pagan worship. The work was doubtless executed by the monks of Paderborn, who were responsible for the organization of the pilgrimages.

One of the oldest surviving examples of carved door panels, this kind of work is Byzantine in origin, but here the style, which is quite simplified but at the same time expressive and animated, is already Romanesque in spirit. ▶

Mary Magdalen (?), detail of an Entombment. c. 1100. Stucco relief. Abbey church of Sankt Cyriakus, Gernrode (Saxony-Anhalt) ▶

Virgin and Child in Majesty. Mid-twelfth century. Stucco. Cathedral of Erfurt (Thuringia)

These rigid and hieratic figures are part of an altarpiece, one of the earliest examples of the sculptured altar decoration which was to become of such importance in the Gothic era.

The monastery of Gernrode is one of the great ecclesiastical centers of Germany. It contains a replica of the Holy Sepulcher adorned with figures in low relief which have an extraordinary psychological intensity in spite of their rather rudimentary technique. This figure probably represents Mary Magdalen standing before the tomb, her gaze blurred by tears. ▶

◀ *Apostle* (detail). c. 1190. Stucco relief. Church of Unsere Liebe Frau, Halberstadt (Saxony-Anhalt)

Saint Andrew. c. 1190. Stucco relief. Church of Unsere Liebe Frau, Halberstadt

The balustrade around the choir at Halberstadt is decorated with figures in relief which are framed by arches. On the north side of the choir enclosure, Christ is surrounded by six Apostles. The seated Saint Andrew, a book held under his arm, shows the considerable progress made by Romanesque sculptors in modeling plastically the folds of garments or the features of an expressive and lifelike face. These reliefs belong to the last stage before the Gothic style of sculpture. In 1962 four successive layers of paint, which had coated over the fine modeling, were removed. With the unveiling of the original dark colors, of which traces remain, the reliefs have regained all their tone and delicacy.

The Fall of Man. End of twelfth century. Ceiling painting. Conventual church of Sankt Michael, Hildesheim ▶

The tapestry below is one of the oldest preserved in Germany, and its composition recalls a manuscript illumination or a Byzantine mosaic.

Saint Michael Slaying the Dragon. Mid-twelfth century. Tapestry. Cathedral Museum, Halberstadt

The paintings on the ceiling of the great church of Sankt Michael go back to the time when the original building, constructed at the beginning of the eleventh century, underwent considerable restoration. There are scenes from the Bible and also figures of saints, all of which are enclosed within medallions or quatrefoils. The Garden of Eden is evoked symbolically by highly stylized trees with the evil serpent coiled around the trunk of the one in the center. The naked figures of Adam and Eve stand out against a starry background. The composition and its style bring to mind any number of miniatures in illuminated Bibles of the time. The colors as we see them now have been restored.

Wall paintings in the Benedictine monastery church of Sankt Georg, Prüfening, near Regensburg (Bavaria). Twelfth century ▶

Wall paintings are infrequent in German Romanesque art, hence the importance of those in Prüfening. The interior of the church is covered with paintings arranged on several levels and laid out in processions of rather monotonous figures in a markedly rigid style.

The paintings in the choir of the convent church on the hill of Nonnberg are of half-length figures of saints set in semicircular niches. The style is very Byzantinesque and the use of color limited, but the drawing of the face shows that the artist was already aiming at expressiveness.

A Saint. Mid-twelfth century. Wall painting. Church of the Benedictine convent of Unserer Lieben Frau Himmelfahrt und Sankt Erentraud, on the Nonnberg, Salzburg (Austria)

MISERERE NOBIS

◀ *The Virgin Mary and Saint Walburga*, detail of the altarpiece of Sankt Walpurgis, Soest (Westphalia). c. 1188. Tempera on panel, over-all height 39″. Landesmuseum für Kunst- und Kulturgeschichte, Münster

Emperor Frederick Barbarossa with His Sons King Henry and Count Frederick, illustration in the *Welfenchronik* from the monastery of Weingarten. 1179–91. Miniature, 12 5/8 × 8 5/8″. Ms. D II, fol. d., Landesbibliothek, Fulda

These portraits—if so they can be called—as also the figures on the very early panel painting (facing page), retain all the rigidity of the Byzantine style. It is difficult to find in them any individuality of features.

Cross of the Abbess Matilda. ▶ Beginning of eleventh century. Wood covered with gold leaf, gilded copper, filigree, precious stones, antique cameos, pearls, and enamels, height 17 3/4″. Treasury of the minster, Essen

Reliquary from the convent of Sankt Vitus at Hochelten, near Düsseldorf. c. 1170–80. Gold and champlevé enamels, with figurines carved from walrus tusks, 21 1/2 × 20 1/8″. Victoria & Albert Museum, London

One of the masterpieces of the goldsmiths' workshops of Cologne, the reliquary is in the form of a centrally planned building in Eastern style with a cupola.

The treasury of the minster at Essen contains some of the most considerable goldsmiths' work in Germany ▶ dating from the Ottonian and Pre-Romanesque periods. It was during the time that Matilda (973–1011), sister of Count Otto of Swabia and Bavaria, was abbess of the convent of Sankt Maria, Cosmas, und Damian (now the minster) that three celebrated processional crosses were executed. The most elaborate of them is that seen here, the only one to present the figure of the crucified Christ in relief.

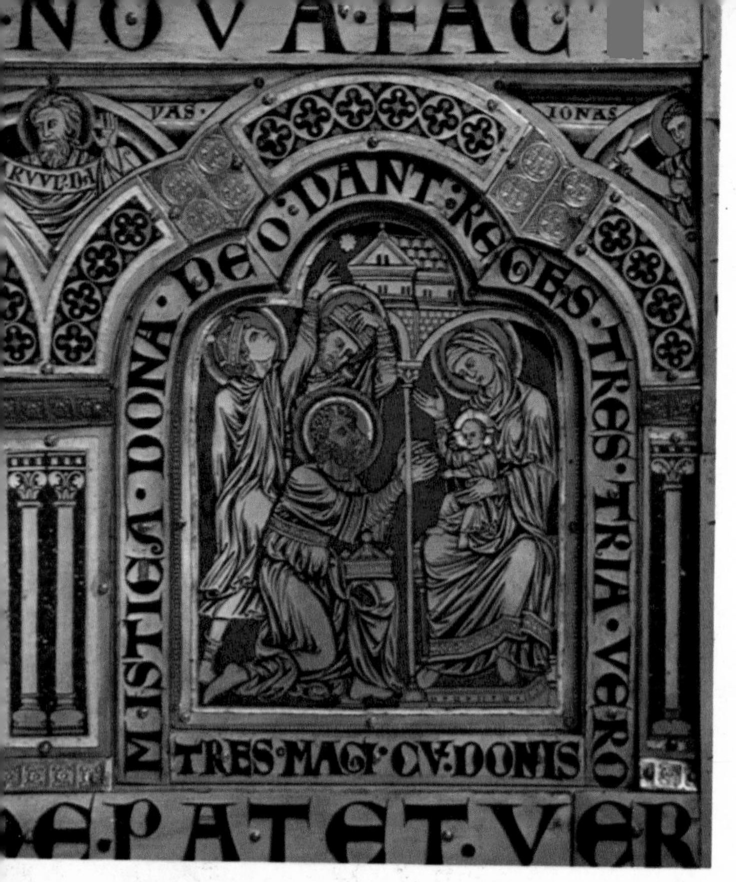

NICHOLAS OF VERDUN (doc. 1181–1205). *Adoration of the Magi*, plaque on an altarpiece. 1181. Champlevé enamel on gold, height $5^{1}/_{2}$″. Chapel of Margrave Leopold the Holy, collegiate church, Klosterneuburg, near Vienna

The fifty-six enamel plaques of the famous altarpiece of Klosterneuburg were once the decoration on an ambo. The Augustinian canons commissioned the work from the great goldsmith Nicholas of Verdun, who had been trained in the Mosan workshops and whose figurative style carried to far-distant abbeys the influence of the sculptural art of Chartres and Saint-Denis, and thereby played a role in the diffusion of the Gothic style.

Often on Romanesque bronze doors one finds this type of door knocker, made up of a lion's head with a ring held in the mouth. The motif itself came from the Middle East.

It was probably the goldsmith-monk Rogerus of Helmarshausen who was responsible for the portable altar below, as he was also for that in the cathedral of the same city. His style is representative of a classicizing trend, based on the imitation of Antique sources, which appeared around 1100.

Door knocker. Twelfth century. Bronze. Church of the Benedictine convent of Sankt Maria, Frauenchiemsee (Bavaria)

ROGERUS OF HELMARSHAUSEN, attributed. Portable altar from the former monastery of Abdinghof. c. 1100. Cut-out, gilded, engraved, and incised laminated copper, height $4^{3}/_{4}$″, width $12^{1}/_{4}$″, depth $7^{1}/_{8}$″. Franciscan monastery, Paderborn

Scandinavia was not untouched by the artistic currents of the Christian West. Found there, among other art objects, are the *Gyldne Altre*, the "golden altars" which are made up of an altar frontal combined with an altarpiece, the latter in the form of a narrow low relief surmounted by a semicircular arch. One of the most complete and earliest of these was done for Lisbjerg. It was made at Aarhus in the twelfth century, although the central crucifix is of an earlier date. The work was executed in chased copper, and a brown varnish was used on the ornamental parts. The figures arranged under arches are separated from each other by bands covered with inscriptions or geometrical motifs. In all the decorative elements (see detail, right), the traditions of Viking art remained still very strong, but the style of the figures came from England. England was, in fact, the principal source of artistic influences affecting Scandinavia, with Germany following in second place.

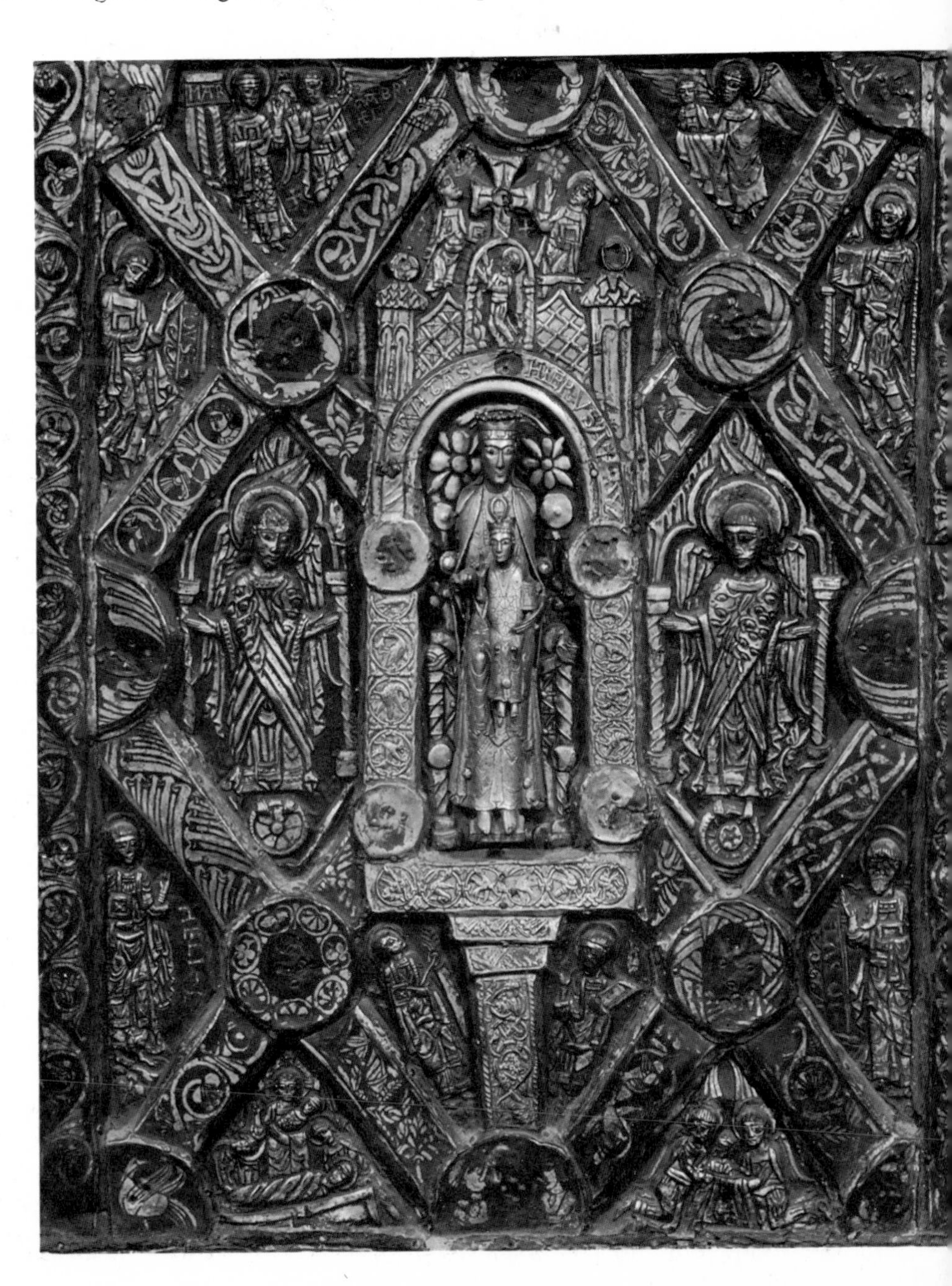

The Golden Altar of Lisbjerg, and detail (right). c. 1140. Chased and gilded laminated copper with gold designs on burnt varnish ground, height c. 8′. Nationalmuseet, Copenhagen

The Madonna of Mosjö (Sweden). Second half of twelfth century. Limewood with original paintwork, height 28″. Statens Historiska Museum, Stockholm

Likewise traceable to direct influence from England is this freestanding statue, whose facial features are reduced to barest essentials but are none the less impressive. The rather peculiar design of the dress, as well as such details as the long plaits of hair and the knot-work pattern in the head covering, are found in English manuscript miniatures of this period, and it is likely that the sculptor used such miniatures as his model. The seated Virgins in Majesty are quite different in style from the Virgins in Majesty done in the twelfth century in France and Germany, indicating that the Nordic lands had certain truly original native traits.

The sources of influence on Scandinavian architecture are quite diverse. The cathedral of Roskilde, burial place of the royal dynasty and the most beautiful religious edifice in Denmark, owes much to the first great Gothic cathedrals of northern France and to the cathedral at Tournai. The bishops who initiated and carried through its construction had resided for long periods in France, and they brought from there ideas for their church and perhaps even a master mason to direct the work. The borrowed elements are easily recognized. The design of the exterior is indebted chiefly to Tournai. The interior, with its characteristic elevation and its tribune, owes something to Noyon and Laon. The great difference is that, here, the cathedral was built in brick, and it is evidence of the very early introduction of the Gothic style into the northernmost countries of Europe.

Cathedral of Roskilde (Zealand, Denmark). 1175–1220

Cathedral of Lund (Sweden). 1103–40

German architecture provided the principal models for the builders of the cathedral at Lund, the most complete and imposing of the Romanesque edifices in Sweden. In design, it is a basilica covered by a timbered ceiling with a transept and a choir which ends in a semicircular apse. The façade has a pair of massive towers pierced by arched openings. The crypt has much in common with that of the cathedral of Speyer. As for the architectonic ornamentation of the exterior of the church (for example the dwarf gallery surmounting the apse), it too, like the articulation of the interior, is related to the churches of the Lower Rhine in particular or, in any case, to those of the Rhineland. However, the rich invention of forms and structures of those German churches is lacking here.

NORMAN ART IN SICILY

Cathedral of Cefalù (Palermo, Sicily). 1131–mid-thirteenth century

In Sicily, at the opposite end of the continent, Romanesque art was impregnated with many and diverse influences: that of Byzantium, whose architects and mosaicists found there a fruitful field for their work; that of Normandy and England by reason of the conquest of Sicily by a Norman dynasty; and that of the Arabs, who for so long had been the ruling power there. In 1131 King Roger II ordered that a cathedral be built in Cefalù to hold his family's tombs. The severe, slender forms of the exterior of the apse and transept recall the great Anglo-Norman cathedrals and abbey churches, and the two towers of the west front, which were added a little later, reveal the same origin. By contrast, the interior is decorated with splendid Byzantine mosaic work.

Apse of the cathedral of Santa Maria la Nuova, Monreale (Palermo). Last quarter of twelfth century ▶

It was also as a royal burial place that King William II began, in 1174, the most immense Romanesque edifice in Sicily. The richness of its decoration is evident even from the outside, in particular on the outer walls of the three apses which round out the choir. Conspicuous here are the interlacing arches, a motif widely used throughout this region. Stringcourses, rose windows, and friezes also contribute to this luxuriant decoration.

BONANNO PISANO (active 1173–c. 1200). *Adam and Eve in the Garden of Eden.* 1185. Bronze relief plaque on the Great Door of the cathedral, Monreale

◀ There are two pairs of bronze doors at Monreale Cathedral. The one on the lateral façade, the work of Barisano of Trani, was done entirely under Byzantine inspiration. The other, on the main portal, is the work of the Pisan artist who also created bronze doors for the cathedral of his native city. Bonanno's art was far more original, more independent of the style of Constantinople, the center which for long had exercised a virtual monopoly in the design and execution of bronze doors. Here the Pisan artist created genuine low reliefs whose scenes, often containing several figures, show a praiseworthy effort in composition despite occasional clumsiness.

The magnificence of the Romanesque Norman art of Sicily blazes forth in the interior of Monreale Cathedral. The fundamental design is a basilica plan, with simple structure and forms, but it is decorated with a dazzling display of opulence, in the large sculptured capitals which crown the magnificent columns of the great arcades as well as in the elegant craftsmanship of the wooden ceiling. But the lavishness of the decoration is expressed, above all, in the extraordinary mosaics which stretch resplendently across the walls of the nave, transept, and choir. In the subtleness of their design, the ingenuity of their composition, and the sumptuousness of their colors, these constitute one of the summits of the mosaic art.

Interior, cathedral of Santa Maria la Nuova, Monreale. Second half of twelfth century

Capitals in the cloister of Monreale Cathedral. End of twelfth century

Along the south wall of Monreale Cathedral stretches a large cloister. It is certain that many sculptors took part in its decoration. Some of them allowed their fantasy to produce figures and scenes which are free interpretations of themes from Antiquity, even tending to a certain imaginative grotesquerie. Here the traditions of Mediterranean Antiquity joined with Romanesque imagination to create a world with all the fantasy of dreams and all the animation of life.

Cloister, Monreale Cathedral. Second half of twelfth century

With its elegant colonnade around a fountain, this is the loveliest part of the cloister. A conscious concern with refinement is evident in the high bases with their multiple moldings, as well as in the highly varied geometrical designs in mosaic which ornament the contours of the shafts of the double columns. All in all, it is an Arabian Nights' dream of Nordic princes, enamored of display and beauty, who were able to command the finest artists and to achieve a harmonious and original blending of many diverse artistic traditions.

Church of San Cataldo, Palermo. Second half of twelfth century

When looking at these bulbous cupolas and horseshoe arches, one cannot help thinking that, surely, the new Norman rulers must have made great use of the Arab artisans and architects who remained in large numbers in this land which was once Moslem, adapting their native style of construction to Christian purposes. The small church of San Cataldo was founded in 1161 by the High Admiral Maione, a citizen of Bari on the mainland. The nave and aisles are of equal height and the building has a peculiar resemblance to the typical Apulian churches with their three cupolas. But its very Oriental exterior remains as evidence of the fascination exercised by Moslem architecture on the new inhabitants of Sicily.

The church seen in the background has a series of cupolas like those of San Cataldo. It was begun in 1132, making use of the vestiges of a mosque. The adjacent cloister is no rival of that at Monreale in richness, but it has the same sort of double columns lined up in rows, and the concentric bands edging the arcades lend a special note of animation to the wall above them. Once again, we see that Romanesque art seems to have had no difficulty in assimilating the forms of the Middle East.

Cloister of the church of San Giovanni degli Eremiti, Palermo. Second quarter of twelfth century

◀ Imperial eagle. Thirteenth–fourteenth centuries, appliquéd on a sixteenth-century altar frontal set with pearls and embroidered in gold thread and silk. Gold, enamel, and semiprecious stones. Cathedral Treasury, Palermo

The Imperial eagle on the facing page is a lasting reminder of the epic story of the German Emperors, which took them as far as southern Italy and the Kingdom of Sicily.

Tomb of Emperor Frederick II Hohenstaufen, and (below) one of the lions supporting the sarcophagus in the tomb. c. mid-thirteenth century. Porphyry and white marble. Cathedral, Palermo

In the thirteenth century Sicily went through a time of political instability as a result of the Imperial ambitions. Frederick II was enchanted by this land, in which he died and was buried, his ambitions disappointed in great part and himself far from the homeland of his German ancestors. Curiously, his funerary monument was designed in imitation of the tomb of his Norman predecessor Roger II, another man of the North who succumbed to the charms of the Mediterranean world. The lid of the sarcophagus is decorated with medallions framing the Imperial eagles, and the urn is supported by lions. The aedicula is capped by a triangular pediment resting on slender columns. In all of these is revealed an overt effort to return to Antique models

Just outside Syracuse, on the road to Catania, lies the small church of San Giovanni alle Catacombe, part of whose west wall dates from early-medieval times. Inside, a staircase leads down to the cruciform crypt of Saint Marcianus where there are traces of old wall paintings and extremely simple architectonic elements. Close by the church is the entrance to extensive catacombs which, in size and scale, far surpass the much better-known catacombs of Rome.

Crypt of Saint Marcianus, Church of San Giovanni alle Catacombe, outskirts of Syracuse

Church of the Trinità, Delia, near Castelvetrano (Trapani). Mid-twelfth century

This little church in southwestern Sicily is a harmonious epitome of the so-called Norman style, of which so many examples, modest or magnificent, can be found in all the regions of the island. Most admirable are the subtle play of volumes interlocking one with the other and the variety of surfaces, some flat, some curved, as in the triple apse and the rounded cupola which tops the edifice. Wall decoration is limited to unobtrusive arches framing the windows. Here everything speaks of a harmonious discretion in which every element is organized in perfect proportions.

◀ In the twelfth century, southern Italy and Sicily enjoyed an extraordinary production of church furnishings in mosaic, the decoration of which was sometimes figurative, sometimes in geometrical designs derived from both Byzantine and Arabic sources. Sculpture in the round, however, as can be seen in these figures of atlantes supporting the pulpit, was directly inspired by ancient Roman statuary.

Exceptional in its design, this apse is conceived as if it were really a façade. The convex central part therefore corresponds to the nave, the flat extensions at either side to the aisles. The entire façade is unified horizontally by a continuous arcade on the intermediate story, and vertically by the employment of the same sort of arcades on the ground floor of the central part and around the drum of the cupola which crowns the edifice. Once again the result is unification and harmony.

◀ Ambo (detail). c. 1175. Marble with colored marble mosaic and gold inlay. Cathedral of San Matteo, Salerno (Campania)

Apse, church of the Annunziata dei Catalani, Messina (Sicily). Twelfth century ▼

Tympanum of the main portal, abbey of San Clemente a Casauria,
Torre de' Passeri (Abruzzi). Second half of twelfth century. Marble

ROMANESQUE ART IN ITALY

A very old Imperial foundation, this abbey owes its west portal to Abbot Leonatus (1152–92). On the low reliefs of the tympanum and lintel is related the history of the monastery. One sees, for example, Abbot Leonatus kneeling before Pope Clement, the sainted patron of the church, and presenting to him a model of the building. Inscriptions identify the principal persons or explain the action of the scenes. The style is quite heavy, the figures squat and thick, their hands crudely carved. Nevertheless, there is a certain narrative feeling in this sculpture, in which one is tempted to discern a faint echo of Burgundian Romanesque art. Interestingly enough, the purely decorative elements—rosettes of acanthus fronds, friezes, stylized foliage around the tympanum and lintel—are treated with greater finesse.

The basilica at Bari contains the highly venerated relics of Saint Nicholas, whence its importance as a church and its imposing dimensions. At the back of the choir, behind the high altar and protected by a fine baldachin, stands the old episcopal throne, a work which is of interest not only for its harmonious proportions and the richness of its sculpture but also because of an inscription commemorating a naval victory won over the Saracen infidels, which gives a clue to its date. The seat is supported on the backs of two half-naked prisoners who grimace with pain, and between them there is a helmeted warrior as a symbol of the Christian victors. The figures give evidence of a quite startling expressionism, and they may perhaps be the work of a Burgundian artist.

Episcopal throne of Archbishop Elia. c. 1098. Marble. Basilica of San Niccolò, Bari (Apulia)

Abbot Desiderius Offering the Model of His Church. After 1073. Detail of a wall painting. Apse of the basilica of Sant'Angelo in Formis, near Capua (Campania)

The imposing ensemble of frescoes that decorate the nave and apse in this church, isolated in the countryside, are of supreme importance in the history of wall painting in Italy. They were due to the initiative of the ecclesiastic who built the church, Desiderius, Abbot of Monte Cassino from 1058 to 1087, and are the work of Benedictine monks trained in the Byzantine style. Monte Cassino, together with Venice, was in fact one of the main routes by which Byzantine art was diffused in the West. Thus, Byzantine influence is evident in the very linear style, the composition, the treatment of the drapery, and the over-all spirit of the paintings. The important point is that a great ensemble of monumental paintings came into existence here and slowly but surely gave rise to a movement which was to become of vast importance in the art of Italy.

Virgin and Child. c. 1220. Polychromed wood, height 42½″. Museo del Palazzo di Venezia, Rome

This statue of a Madonna, which comes from Acuto near Agnani in Latium, is not only painted but is also embellished with cabochons, as reliquary statues were. The hieratic style of Byzantium is attenuated here by an effort at naturalism which comes more from Antique statuary (even now in Latium there are numerous vestiges of ancient Rome) than from the intrusion of a Gothic influence which, at that time, had hardly made itself felt as yet in this region of Italy. The particular feeling of animation which marks this group is due in part to the gesture of the Christ child, pointing upward.

Abbey of Santa Maria, Pomposa (Emilia). First third of eleventh century

One of the unique features of Italian architecture was the isolated bell tower, the campanile, and it continued so right up to the Renaissance. At Pomposa, a powerful abbey of ancient foundation, a porch was added to the church at the beginning of the eleventh century. This narthex is pierced by three arches and decorated with varicolored stones and low reliefs. The church itself is rather overshadowed by the mass of the imposing bell tower, which is made up of several stories decorated by bands in the Lombard manner and lit by openings that increase in number from bottom to top.

The towers of San Gimignano (Tuscany). Twelfth–fourteenth centuries

These strange towers with their grimly bare walls are the remains of the fortified palaces which powerful families erected in the cities of medieval Italy as a kind of gesture of defiance to the limitations of brick and stone. They seem to anticipate, in a curious way, the American skyscraper.

Façade, basilica of San Michele, Pavia (Lombardy). Second half of twelfth century ▶

Detail of the sculptured decoration on the façade of the church of San Pietro, Spoleto (Umbria). Thirteenth century. Travertine

Nothing remains of the old thirteenth-century church in Spoleto except the façade, hanging like a tapestry of delicately carved low reliefs which are arranged on several levels to frame and surmount the portal. Displayed on it is an extraordinary repertory of decorative motifs of the greatest variety in both design and the technique of relief carving. Of truly admirable quality is the flowing vigor of the foliated scrolls that frame the portal, and also the infinite variations of lacework that mantle the wall between tiny colonnettes which support arches or architraves. There is also a veritable bestiary with both monstrous and real animals. The peacock pecking at a bunch of grapes testifies to the qualities of observation of an artist who was in full control of his medium.

The typical northern Italian Romanesque façade, as seen here, is flat and bare, except for a few vertical clustered columns rising the full height of the wall, an occasional frieze or horizontal band of low reliefs, and, crowning all, a blind arcade which follows the line of the peaked roof. The subjects of the low reliefs are mostly scenes of demons, and they are the work of the so-called Comacini, artists who came from Como and who characteristically combined forms borrowed from Antiquity with others native to Lombardy. ▶

Inner court of the castle of Celano (Abruzzi). First half of thirteenth century, with extensive later additions and restorations

High in the mountains at Celano stands a stronghold built by Frederick II. Its rectangular court, surrounded by a double gallery, exemplifies the severe style of architecture which the great Emperor adopted in Italy.

Campanile of the cathedral ▶
of Pisa (Tuscany). Begun 1173

Completely isolated from the cathedral, the campanile was begun in 1173. Construction went slowly, held up over and over again as the terrain subsided under the great weight, whence the inclination which has given the "Leaning Tower" its popular name. Rows of arcades seem to twine around the tower, but their repetition does not create an impression of monotony because they are of several different heights, and the result is, instead, an effect of noble grandeur in this subtle variation on a single theme.

Façade, church of San Frediano, Lucca (Tuscany). Church built 1112–47. Mosaic by Bonaventura Berlinghieri, c. 1260 ▶

BONANNO PISANO. *The Massacre of the Innocents*, bronze relief on the door of San Ranieri, Pisa Cathedral. c. 1190–c. 1200

We have already encountered Bonanno Pisano in connection with one of his earlier works, the bronze door of the cathedral of Monreale in Sicily (see page 166). Here he used the same approach, but with perhaps greater freshness and spontaneity. The artist's new-found desire for simplification rendered human emotion and expression in a more powerful manner, as in this scene where the drama of the Massacre of the Innocents is reduced to the three main personages: Herod, the soldier-executioner, and the weeping mother. It does not matter that the children are no more than shapeless dolls. One feels that, from this point on, the art of Antiquity and its human values would be the continuous inspiration of artists, and that here began the evolution which led at last to Giotto.

The church of San Frediano was built between 1112 and 1147, in the form of a double-aisled basilica, by Tuscan ▶ masters who were deeply inspired by classical Antiquity, as can be seen in the colonnade which extends across the entire façade and is so much like that of an ancient temple. The immense mosaic on the theme of the Ascension which fills the upper part of the façade dates from around 1260 and shows how Byzantine influence continued to hold sway, even at that late date.

ALTAVIRICELI SPECTATVRCORGALILEI
+ISTE DEI NATVS
GALILEINVBELEVATVS

In a continuous frieze around this baptismal font are low reliefs on the theme of the life of Moses. The modeling is fairly succinct and the composition somewhat confused. Nevertheless, there are vigor and animation in this work which was directly inspired by the reliefs on Antique sarcophaguses, down to such fine details as the garments, the way of depicting a tree, and the medallion framing a bust. At the time the font was done, there were workshops of sculptors in Pisa, near Lucca, whose products were in demand in far-distant places.

Baptistery of San Giovanni, Florence (Tuscany). c. 1060–1150 ▶

Baptismal font. Mid-twelfth century. Church of San Frediano, Lucca

As so often in this epoch, the baptistery in Florence is a separate building, detached from the cathedral. It is built on a central plan as a regular octagon and is crowned by a cupola concealed beneath a peaked, tentlike roof. The flat exterior walls are enlivened by arcades on the middle story, but even more effectively by the harmonious combination of different colored marbles, which lend a note of lightness to this compact architecture. The Florence baptistery, one of the largest and most beautiful to survive, was later to play a vital role in the history of sculpture in the Renaissance, when Lorenzo Ghiberti created his celebrated reliefs for the bronze doors.

◀ Nave, church of San Miniato al Monte, Florence. Interior completed 1062

San Miniato, the church of a Benedictine monastery, has an elevated choir above a crypt which opens directly into the nave. Varicolored marbles are used as decoration both inside and out. The entire interior is covered by an open timberwork ceiling and is given a regular rhythm by diaphragm arches which rest on piers composed of four half columns. Between these run the lateral arcades supported by columns. The over-all impression is of ample volume and harmonious articulation of the interior. The marble mosaic in the pavement dates from 1207.

One of the most imposing monastic constructions of northern Italy is the basilica in Verona. Its choir is raised above a crypt which is reached through a triple arch richly decorated with delicate low reliefs. The high, severe nave is covered with a timberwork ceiling, done in Gothic style in the 1380s, which is supported by diaphragm arches. The semicircular arches of the great lateral arcades rest on an alternation of compound bridge piers and columns. The only light enters through a few small windows, so that the interior is always in shadow.

Nave, basilica of San Zeno Maggiore, Verona (Veneto). 1125–78

The Expulsion from Paradise, bronze plaque in low relief on the wooden doors of the basilica of San Zeno Maggiore, Verona. c. 1100

The great door of San Zeno Maggiore is decorated with low reliefs in bronze, the earliest of which go back to 1100. The Biblical scenes are crude and archaic, but they were the first groping attempts to rediscover the art of bronze relief whose traditions had been lost, at least in northern Italy.

In the Germanic countries, too, there were sculptors who cast metal. The origin of the doors at Novgorod is ▶ much disputed: the latest hypothesis is that, commissioned by the Polish Bishop of Plock, they were executed at Magdeburg and then purchased by merchants from Novgorod as a gift for their cathedral. Scenes from both Testaments are presented in square plaques, except at the top, and these are separated by garlands of stylized foliage. As in Italy, the door handles are held in the mouths of lions.

Cast bronze doors of the cathedral of Sancta Sophia, Novgorod. Second half of twelfth century. Height 11′ 9¾″, combined width 7′ 10½″

Elijah Taken up into Heaven, cast bronze relief on the doors of Sancta Sophia, Novgorod. Height c. $15^{3}/_{4}$″

The style of these low reliefs is rudimentary and naïve, though the scenes are narrated with considerable spontaneity and a sure feeling for the picturesque and lively. One has the impression that the artist, an original personality, preferred to give rein to his fantasy rather than to copy models. Some of the episodes depicted are unusual in Romanesque iconography.

Eve and *Self-Portrait of the Sculptor*, detail of the bronze doors of Sancta Sophia, Novgorod ▶

At the bottom of the left leaf of the door, directly next to the scene of the Fall of Man, the artist portrayed himself, dressed in the fashion of his time and holding the tools of his trade. The same physical type is used for most of the figures in the reliefs. Latin inscriptions and others in Russian in Cyrillic characters were added after the reliefs were cast.

This type of façade is characteristic of the Romanesque churches in northern Italy, with the arch of its deep porch resting on slender colonnettes which rise above crouching lions. To either side of the central portal are friezes which continue across the lintel of the door. There is an obvious parallel here with the church of Saint-Gilles-du-Gard in Provence. Quite remarkably, there are also three-dimensional statues in niches set into the walls. Attributed to Benedetto Antelami, they are among the earliest important medieval statues in the round. Antique sources are further recalled by two Corinthian columns which stand in isolation, supporting nothing, at either side of the portal. The same type of façade—sometimes more, sometimes less, imposing—is found in Verona, Modena, and throughout the region.

Portal of the cathedral of Fidenza (Emilia). Twelfth century

BENEDETTO ANTELAMI (c. 1150–c. 1225). *Spring*, from a cycle of statues depicting the seasons and the months. End of twelfth century. White Parma stone. Baptistery of San Giovanni, Parma (Emilia)

The baptistery in Parma represents one of the chief landmarks in the history of sculpture, as regards both reliefs and freestanding statues. It was there that a powerful artistic personality came to light, Benedetto Antelami, of crucial importance in his own right and also as head of a large workshop. Antelami can still be classed as a Romanesque master, although in his last works, such as this elegant figure of a young girl holding an apple in a frightened manner, he was obviously influenced by French Gothic sculpture—in particular that of Chartres, which he no doubt visited. Here one finds the same economy of means, notable in the drapery, the same noble elegance and humanity. Antelami opened the way to the future progress of Italian sculpture, and his influence can be traced in the work of the Pisano family in the latter half of the thirteenth century.

Nave, basilica of Sant'Ambrogio, Milan (Lombardy). Nave c. 1128, vault 1180

Built for an abbey of venerable date, Sant'Ambrogio is vaulted and has a huge cupola over what would be the crossing if there were a transept. The nave is flanked by double bays surmounted by a gallery whose large semicircular openings have the same diameter as the great main arches. All in all, it is a remarkable example of a Lombard church, its vast interior producing an impression of austere but calm strength. In the choir can be seen the baldachin raised over the high altar and behind it, in the apse, a mosaic in Byzantine style.

Detail of the apse, basilica of Sant'Abbondio, Como (Lombardy). 1063–95

Begun in 1063, consecrated by the Pope in 1095, Sant' Abbondio is one of the great religious edifices of Italy, remarkable not only for its dimensions and proportions (its nave is flanked by double aisles) but also for the majestic articulation of the ensemble. But the Lombards were more than master builders. It was in Como and its vicinity that were also found the workshops of sculptors whose activities often took them to far-distant places, to Germany even. They were particularly gifted at reliefs, which they carved delicately with nonfigurative motifs such as plaits, knotwork, and foliated scrolls, designs which were derived from Oriental cloths and ivories. Into such abstract ornamentation were also introduced stylized fabulous monsters. It must not be forgotten that Lombard architecture and sculpture were of enormous influence in the formation and evolution of Romanesque art.

Cloister of the monastery of San Cugat del Vallés (Barcelona).
End of twelfth and beginning of thirteenth centuries

ROMANESQUE ART IN SPAIN

Romanesque architecture flourished remarkably in the northern regions of the Iberian Peninsula, most notably in Catalonia which had close ties to nearby Languedoc. In Spain, the Romanesque style lasted well into the Gothic period. If the second story of the cloister in the important abbey of San Cugat belongs to the Gothic, the galleries of the ground floor, with their powerful semicircular arches resting on twinned colonnettes, mark the apogee of the Romanesque. The name of the sculptor or master of works is known, Arnaldus Gatell, a Catalan name which the monk himself signed on a capital. His capitals are in a very beautiful and elaborate style, whether they have figures or merely foliage designs.

Cloister of the cathedral of Tarragona. Twelfth–thirteenth centuries

Majestic and complex as this great cathedral now appears, its present aspect is the product of several stages of construction. Of special note is the *cimborio*, the lantern tower over the crossing, which is characteristic of most churches of this period. Elements such as the bell tower and the small apse on the north arm of the transept are Gothic additions, but are integrated without conflict into the austere and noble Romanesque structure. Among the most beautiful creations of Romanesque art in Spain are the cloisters, and it is in them that are found the most important ensembles of sculpture. Those seen here date from late Romanesque times.

Cloister of the monastery of Poblet (Tarragona). Thirteenth century

Nave, abbey church of Poblet. ▶ Twelfth–thirteenth centuries

Poblet and Santas Creus are the great Cistercian monasteries of Catalonia. At Poblet the cloisters, with their ogival-vaulted passageways, are almost entirely Gothic. However, the oldest section, immediately adjoining the church (to the right in this photograph), retains Romanesque traits, especially in its round arches resting on small double columns. In accord with Cistercian principles, decoration consists only of stylized foliage.

The church was begun in the second half of the twelfth century in Romanesque style, the Gothic making only ▶ a furtive appearance in the aisles and transept. The nave is covered by a slightly pointed barrel vault with a rhythmic succession of transverse ribs resting on engaged columns which are interrupted before they reach the ground. Arched windows without any ornamentation pierce the walls above the great lateral arcades. Tall relieving arches rise up to the stringcourse which marks the beginning of the vault. Seven chapels radiate from the ambulatory around the apse. Certainly, the severity and nobility of this architecture owe much to the austere principles of the Cistercians.

◄ Cloister of the cathedral of Santa Maria, Gerona. Twelfth century

The Fall of Man, low relief on a pier in the southern passageway of the cloister at Gerona. Second half of twelfth century

The Garden of Eden is represented by shrubs which have only the vaguest resemblance to grapevines. Satan in reptilian form coils around the branches, while to either side are Adam and Eve, their nakedness concealed by vine leaves. Their bodies are thick, with disproportionately large heads, and the figures are modeled in an almost primitive manner.

◄ Alongside the cathedral at Gerona, which was reconstructed in the fourteenth and fifteenth centuries, there remains the old Romanesque cloister. Its round arches with concave moldings rest on a double row of colonnettes whose capitals are, for the most part, sculpted with either foliage or fabulous animals, some face to face, others back to back. The pillars of the southern gallery are ornamented with narrative friezes which depict episodes from the Old Testament in a somewhat sketchy and archaic style.

◀ Nave of the monastic church of San Pedro de Roda (Gerona). Eleventh century

Monastery of San Pedro de Roda. Consecrated 1022

Here is a monument which is exceptional as much because of its situation on the top of an arid, uninhabited mountain as for its architecture and sculpture. The church was consecrated as early as 1022, and yet its nave and aisles, transept, and ambulatory clearly reveal an astonishing and even precocious scientific understanding of forms and architectonic arrangement. The semicircular barrel vault over the nave is supported by transverse ribs which rest on two superposed columns. The lower column, which stands on a high pedestal, is on the same level and has the same dimensions as the column that bears the weight of the semicircular arches of the pier arcades. The capitals have remarkable sculpture, done in the marble workshops which, in the Pyrenees region, remained in operation for so long after the period of the Barbarian invasions.

Cloister of the church of Santa María, Estany (Barcelona). Consecrated 1133, some sculpture of later date

Like most Catalan cloisters, these—which are extremely large compared with the church against which they were built—have double rows of narrow columns, all of which have sculptured capitals. What is remarkable is that this sculpture continued to cling faithfully to the Romanesque style well into the fourteenth century. This is seen in the figured capitals, which have much in common with folk art, as well as in those whose bells are covered with twining forms and stylized motifs in the purest Romanesque tradition. Such persistence of the Romanesque style, in both decoration and architecture, is not unusual in the Iberian Peninsula.

The numerous capitals with figures in these cloisters date from several different periods, but they all belong to a folk tradition which remained stubbornly archaic and poor in inspiration. They illustrate scenes from the Old and New Testaments in an arrangement which seems to follow no decipherable order or program. In the least crude of them, such as the Last Supper, the figures are a little monotonous. To cover the bell of the capital, the sculptor could find no other solution than to arrange the Apostles in two rows, and they are indistinguishable one from the other, except for the Saint John whose head rests on Christ's breast.

In the cloister of the abbey at Vilabertrán (facing ▶ page), the arcades are alternately supported by twinned columns and rectangular piers. Most of the capitals are quite simple, decorated with large, highly stylized leaves which seem to anticipate Gothic ornamental forms. This would seem to place the date of the cloister toward the end of the twelfth century, but the massiveness of its structure relates it beyond doubt to the Romanesque.

▲
Capitals in the cloister at Estany. Stone, $19^1/_2 \times 11 \times 11''$ ▶

Facing page: cloister of the abbey of Santa María, Vilabertrán (Gerona). Twelfth century

Church of San Clemente, Tahull (Lérida). Twelfth century

South portal, called *Porta dels Fillols*, old cathedral, Lérida. Thirteenth century ▶

The church, consecrated in 1123, is made up of a nave and aisles to which, on the exterior, correspond the principal and the two minor apses. The interior is not vaulted but roofed over with a pitched wooden ceiling, a solution which is quite exceptional in Catalonia. Another notable feature is the bell tower to one side, almost detached from the church in the manner of Lombard campaniles and using the same system of enlarging the openings from the base to the top of the tower. Tahull is, in fact, a characteristic example of what has been called Southern Early Romanesque art, a widespread style marked by quite definite similarities between the religious edifices of northern Italy and northern Spain.

Though built in the thirteenth century at the same time as the church, the portals at Lérida remained strictly faithful to the Romanesque decorative forms. The *Porta dels Fillols* (Portal of the Kings' Sons), which opens into the middle of the south aisle, is the most sumptuous of them. Its five concentric archivolts are covered with a diversity of geometrical motifs: foliated scrolls, zigzags, interlacing semicircles, sawteeth, and bead-and-reel moldings. There is no tympanum, and the moldings all terminate on the capitals of slender columns and pilasters. The capitals are composed of foliated scrolls and plaitwork, in the coils of which appear fantastic beasts. Here, then, is another example of the obstinate persistence of Romanesque art south of the Pyrenees.

Monastery of Santa María, Ripoll. First consecration 977, further building begun 1020, second consecration 1032. Entirely rebuilt 1887

In the foreground, crowned by the lantern tower, is the immense transept off which spring one principal and six minor apses. Inside, the nave and four aisles are surmounted by a wooden beamed ceiling. Unfortunately the present building is no more than a faithful reconstruction of the original which was destroyed when the Carlists set fire to it in 1835. The entire east end of the edifice was built at the beginning of the eleventh century by the great Abbot Oliba, who was celebrated as much for his culture as for his building activities.

◀ Façade, abbey church of Santa María, Ripoll (Gerona). Twelfth century

The façade here is a solid wall of sculptured reliefs, making up one of the most remarkable and most impressive ensembles of Romanesque sculpture that exists. Tragically, the sculpture was severely damaged by fire in the nineteenth century. The reliefs are arranged in several tiers around the portal, which is itself emphasized by a series of decorative parallel moldings. The richness of the iconography of these reliefs, which is explained by the high intellectual level of this monastic center, is unmatched elsewhere and still baffles modern scholars. The models imitated can be found for the most part in the so-called Bible of Ripoll, now in the Vatican Library.

◀ Nave, collegiate church of San Vicente, in the castle of Cardona (Barcelona). 1019–40

Cupola over the crossing, collegiate church of San Vicente, Cardona

◀ Perched on a mountaintop, the church at Cardona is one of the most perfect creations of Southern Early Romanesque art. Its nave is covered with a barrel vault whose transverse ribs rest on the projections of massive pillars without capitals. The great compound arches rise to a considerable height, while higher still the walls are pierced by windows. The raised choir can be seen, beneath which lies the crypt.

The transept is not conspicuous, but the crossing is crowned by a cupola resting on squinches. Sunlight pours in through an opening at the summit and also through small rectangular apertures in one half only of the cupola. As early as the start of the eleventh century, the first Romanesque builders had already arrived at satisfactory solutions to the problems of vaulting, which they employed to give their interiors a remarkable feeling of spaciousness.

Christ in Majesty, detail of a wall painting ▶ formerly covering the entire apse of San Clemente, Tahull. Dated December 10, 1123. Museo de Bellas Artes de Cataluña, Barcelona

The Entombment of Saint Thomas of Canterbury. End of twelfth century. Wall painting in a minor apse of the church of Santa María, Tarrasa (Barcelona)

The frescoes of the churches of Tahull (see page 214) are very representative of Catalan painting: harshly vigorous, highly linear, with compositions which are painstakingly worked out but are, all told, a little monotonous. The great upsurge of wall painting in Catalonia was due to Italian influence, the art of nearby France affecting only its decorative style.

At Tarrasa there survives a group of three churches of worthy age, their oldest parts being incorporated into constructions of the early Romanesque period. Wall paintings are found throughout Catalonia, and at Tarrasa there is a cycle devoted to the life of Saint Thomas of Canterbury, who was martyred in 1170 by order of King Henry II of England and was canonized three years later. His cult spread with astonishing rapidity throughout Western Christendom. The cycle at Tarrasa, evidence of the widespread popularity of the new saint, is painted with elegance, even a little preciously, in a style of precise contours and sinuous lines. As is common in Romanesque iconography, the soul is seen leaving the dead body in the shape of a little figure, its hands in a gesture of prayer, which is borne heavenward in a shroud held by two angels.

EGO
LVX
SVM

Virgin and Child. Twelfth century. Polychromed wood, height 21¼″. Museo de Bellas Artes de Cataluña, Barcelona

Catalan sculpture in the round resembles in many ways the wall paintings of that region and, in fact, was generally painted with the same bright, flattish colors. This Madonna has the same hallucinating stare out of strongly outlined eyes which makes the Christ of Tahull such a moving work. Crowned, seated, draped in a mantle which falls in rectilinear folds, she seems as inflexible as an idol.

Crucifix. Twelfth century. Polychromed wood, height of figure 36″. ▶ Museo de Bellas Artes de Cataluña, Barcelona

Crucifixes of this type are frequent in Catalan art. They are called *Majestades* because the Christ, dressed in a long robe, appears more as a God in Majesty, hieratic and remote, than as a sufferer on the Cross. It is possible that this very special type of crucifix, which is also found in other countries, among them Germany (see the example from Brunswick, page 139), goes back to one particular source, the eleventh-century *Volto Santo* effigy in the cathedral of Lucca in Italy. The crucifix seen here, known as the *Majestad Battló*, is distinguished by its brilliant coloring.

Descent from the Cross. Mid-thirteenth century. Wood sculpture. Abbey church of San Juan de las Abadesas (Gerona)

Detail of central part of an altar or tomb frontal from Santo Domingo de Silos (Burgos). Third quarter of twelfth century. Plaques of enameled copper on oak panel with bands of enameled and gilded silver studded with cabochons, total dimensions $33^1/_2 \times 99^1/_2''$. Museo Arqueológico, Burgos ▶

Besides the stone sculpture which decorates the Romanesque churches of northern Spain, there have survived a large number of wooden statues, which are lifesize and usually painted. They show already the taste for violent expressionism which was to be so characteristic of Spanish art in later centuries. Scenes of the Passion, such as this *Descent from the Cross*—one of the most complete to have survived—were frequently depicted. Though consecrated as late as 1251, it still belongs to the purest Romanesque tradition, the reason for this being that it comes from a folk art which was handed down from generation to generation in family workshops.

Among the treasures of the great Spanish monasteries were superb examples of metalwork, some of which ▶ may have been brought in from abroad. The altar frontal from Santo Domingo de Silos in Old Castile was most likely turned out by one of those workshops which supplied painted enamels to all of Christian Europe.

A

Castle of Loarre (Huesca). Eleventh–twelfth centuries

One of the finest examples of those monastery-fortresses so numerous in the Iberian Peninsula, where they were generally built on superb sites, Loarre rises high on a peak at the edge of the Aragonese mountains. The exterior fortified walls are quite well preserved, as are several towers within the ring of walls, and there still stands a chapel with a barrel vault and a semidome in the apse. The differences in masonwork point to several stages of construction extending from the eleventh to the twelfth century.

Cupola of the chapel of the San Sepulcro, Torres del Río (Navarre). Probably end of twelfth century ▶

Spanish architecture shows numerous traces of Moslem influence, and, in fact, many Moslems worked for the Christians after the Reconquest. This may explain the unusual disposition of the tracery of the ribwork in this cupola, and the grooved consoles below the cornice are also probably of Arabic origin.

◀ *The Holy Women at the Sepulcher*, detail of a stone relief on the façade of the church of San Miguel, Estella (Navarre). End of twelfth century

Portal of the church of San Pedro de la Rúa, Estella (Navarre). Twelfth century

◀ The façade of San Miguel in Estella is covered with sculpture in high relief, most notable among which are the series of figures on the walls to either side of the portal. These works are rather rudimentary in modeling, and though they betray some faint influence from the early Gothic art of France, in form and spirit they are still profoundly tied to the Romanesque. Whatever else may be said of them, they do possess a certain expressive sensitivity.

The *rúa* here is the route to Santiago de Compostela. The church of San Pedro de la Rúa is situated in what was the ward of the "Franks," a small colony of foreigners who lived on what they earned from travelers on the great pilgrimage route. Not unexpectedly, therefore, foreign influences can be made out here. The multiple archivolts of this portal are not unlike those of certain churches in the west of France, while the scalloped arch framing the doorway and the motifs that decorate it must derive from Islamic art.

The Marriage Feast at Cana (above) and *The Supper at Emmaus* (facing page), capitals in the cloisters of the collegiate church of Santa María la Mayor, Tudela (Navarre). c. 1186

The collegiate church at Tudela dates mainly from the end of the twelfth century, but the sculptured decoration, and in particular the many capitals of the large cloister, are Romanesque. Most of the scenes are drawn from the Gospels or the lives of saints. There is a certain unity of style in the ample folds of the garments, the large heads with thick features, and the globular eyes. The artist possessed a sure instinct for narration in setting forth his scenes in a lively manner, and his decorative sense can be seen in the foliated scrolls and knotwork of the abacus of these capitals.

West portal, cathedral of Jaca (Huesca). Beginning of twelfth century

Cloister, collegiate church of Santillana del Mar (Santander). End of twelfth century ▶

This tympanum is ornamented with symbolic figures whose significance is still very obscure. The sacred monogram, a symbol which takes the form of a large wheel, is found quite frequently on both sides of the Pyrenees. It is employed as a sign of the Trinity, a principle as perfect in itself as the wheel. Here, to either side of it, are lions, which presumably are images of Christ. At the left, Christ-the-Lion takes pity on the repentant sinner, represented by a man on all fours who struggles with the serpent, symbol of Evil. At the right, Christ-the-Lion triumphs over Death as typified by an asp and a basilisk. Inscriptions on the tympanum provide some clue to this esoteric symbolism. The relief modeling is done with great delicacy, which testifies to the high standard of the school of sculpture working in Jaca.

The church at Santillana was also a halting place on the road to Santiago. The cloister, whose twinned ▶ columns seem somewhat heavy, has an ensemble of capitals which demonstrate what Romanesque art became in its declining period. The decoration consists chiefly of scrollwork and of stylized foliage through which glide fabulous beasts and legendary beings. Although the work is technically competent, one cannot help sensing an over-all lack of inventiveness.

◀ East end of the church of San Lorenzo, Sahagún (León). Begun in thirteenth century

The *Puerta de las Platerías*, cathedral of Santiago de Compostela (Corunna). Beginning of twelfth century

◀ The influence of Arabic architecture is here even more pronounced, so much so that it can be qualified as *Mudéjar*, the Hispano-Moresque style the Arabs bequeathed to Christian Spain; and in fact the exceptionally massive bell tower which rises above the choir was built in brick, as was the practice of Moslem masons.

The *Puerta de las Platerías* (Portal of the Silversmiths' Shops), in the south transept of Santiago Cathedral, is the only one of the original three Romanesque portals that has survived, and it must be said that it seems like a rather odd assemblage of dismembered pieces of sculpture. The portal is composed of two doors, each with a tympanum decorated not only with scenes from the life of Christ but also with mysterious and fascinating figures, among them a woman holding a skull. Flanking the doors are slender marble colonnettes, of which one in each group is carved with tiny figures under arcades. Above the portal and in a narrow strip to either side are a great many figures in low relief arranged at various levels. On the spandrel between the arches of the doors is a very fine half-length figure of Abraham, his hands opened in a gesture difficult to interpret. All of these reliefs are in marble.

Nave, cathedral of Santiago de Compostela. First half of twelfth century

Santiago de Compostela is typical of the grandiose pilgrimage churches. The nave has massive arcades, their great arches supported on compound piers. Above, there is a vast gallery which must have accommodated a good part of the enormous crowds of pilgrims who gathered here. The church is vaulted, has an ambulatory, and over the crossing is a great lantern tower. Such spaciousness and power are found in certain French churches which likewise were great pilgrimage centers, among them Saint-Sernin in Toulouse and Sainte-Foy in Conques.

This relief is set into the west jamb of the left door of the *Puerta de las Platerías*. The seated David, his legs crossed, playing the rebec, is strikingly similar to the women holding the signs of the Lion and the Ram in the relief in Toulouse (see page 15), who have the same pose and the same play of drapery. There are even the same characteristic faults in the joining of arm and shoulder, the arclike bend of the arms, and the excessive length of the feet. These are unimpeachable proof of the artistic relationships between the northern Iberian Peninsula and southwestern France, which resulted from the historical phenomenon of the great pilgrimage routes. There can be no doubt that the carvers of images moved from one place to another along those great axes of Christendom, going wherever there was work to be done.

King David. Beginning of twelfth century. Low relief in stone. Cathedral of Santiago de Compostela

Side portal, collegiate church of San Isidoro, León (detail). Mid-twelfth century

The tympanum here is made up of three slabs of marble placed side by side, each carved in relief with a different subject. In the center is the Descent from the Cross; to the right, the Holy Women at the Sepulcher; to the left, the Ascension. San Isidoro, which was consecrated in 1149, was one of the important halting places along the *camino francés*, the road from France to Santiago de Compostela. It is not surprising, therefore, to discover a close relationship between this portal and the Porte Miégeville of Saint-Sernin in Toulouse. The latter would seem to be earlier, because the sculptor of León appears to have copied its motifs without really understanding their significance. The capitals likewise have analogies with those in Toulouse.

The Annunciation to the Shepherds. Second half of twelfth century. ▶
Painting on the vault of the Royal Pantheon, church of San Isidoro, León

The Royal Pantheon, which was designed as a funerary chapel, contains one of the most complete cycles of mural painting in the whole of the peninsula. It was probably done during the reign of Ferdinando II of León (1157–88). The colors have retained all their freshness through the centuries, and the subtly drawn, highly diversified paintings stand out expressively against their light background. The composition is airy and harmonious and testifies to a real feeling for nature. The artist showed great skill in transferring onto a monumental scale a system of images and decorative motifs which he derived from manuscript illuminations.

ANGE
LVS
PAS
TORES

Funeral monument. End of twelfth or beginning of thirteenth century. Church of La Magdalena, Zamora (León)

Saints Matthew and Philip. End of twelfth century. ▶ Stone statues. Cámara Santa, cathedral of Oviedo

The tomb above is remarkable for its arrangement under a richly decorated baldachin. The dead woman is stretched out on her death bed, while angels carry her soul aloft in a shroud, as is usual in Romanesque iconography. The sculpture and decorative motifs of this monument are Romanesque, but its unusual form places it in a very late period.

In the ninth century, when Oviedo was the capital of the Kingdom of Asturias, a special chapel, the ▶ Cámara Santa, was built to house a treasure of very sacred relics. At the end of the twelfth century the vault was constructed containing statues of the Apostles, the sculptor of which must have known the column statues so frequent in early French churches. His art shows great vigor in the treatment of the draperies, the expressiveness of the faces, and the diversity of posture.

The Annunciation to the Shepherds. End of eleventh century. Plaque of gilded repoussé silver laid over cedarwood, on a reliquary shrine. Cámara Santa, cathedral of Oviedo

Christ in Glory. Another detail from the same reliquary ▶

The Christ in Glory (facing page), right hand raised in blessing, enthroned within a mandorla held by four angels, is the principal motif on the front of a richly decorated reliquary; the scene of the shepherds (above) is on a side panel. The plaques were done in repoussé, a technique in which the design is pressed into relief from the reverse side of a thin sheet of silver. The style is somewhat rigid and awkward, though the artist attempted to lend animation to certain of the scenes, among them that of the Annunciation to the Shepherds. Inscriptions in Arabic Kufic characters comment on the scenes and personages. Whether it was done by Spanish artists or brought in from abroad, this shrine ranks among the masterpieces of the treasure of Oviedo.

◀ This crucifix, with its figure of Christ in very high relief, was made out of three separate pieces. Characteristics such as the head drooping on the shoulder and the wide-open eyes (a common trait in Romanesque Christs) indicate that this is undoubtedly a Spanish work. The arms of the cross are edged by strips of very delicately executed reliefs of fighting animals, which, in the Romanesque way of thinking, symbolize the struggle between Good and Evil.

The fortification of Ávila was begun in 1090 by Alfonso VI, King of Castile. The walls completely encircled the old city, and even today still have a circumference of nearly two miles. They are without doubt the best preserved and most complete of early times. There are no less than eighty-six semicylindrical towers projecting from the walls, and nine fortified gates. Laid out to follow the lines of the terrain, the walls were built from carefully cut blocks of granite and, in some stretches, from bricks. On the almost desertlike plateau of Old Castile, these austere and imposing battlements produce an unforgettable impression.

◀ Crucifix. Before 1163. Museo Arqueológico Nacional, Madrid

The walls of Ávila. Twelfth century

◀ South portal, cathedral of Ciudad Rodrigo (Salamanca). Second half of twelfth century

At the very end of the Spanish Romanesque, the superb cathedral in Ciudad Rodrigo, half-Romanesque, half-Gothic in style, was decorated with statues in which one senses the influence of the first Gothic sculpture in France. This is notable in the large Christ in Majesty flanked by Apostles below the wide arch framing the portal, as well as in the frieze of saints in arched niches which stretches across the upper story in a way similar to the Royal Galleries on the great Gothic façades of northern France. Despite a certain rigidity, these statues are vigorous and expressive in style.

Apse of the old cathedral, Salamanca. Twelfth century

The old cathedral in Salamanca was begun in 1152 on a plan which was still entirely Romanesque, with three semicircular apses which correspond to the nave and aisles. As building progressed, the style changed, as did the technique of construction, which began to follow the Gothic principles in use in southwestern France. Seen here is the main apse with, behind it, the lantern tower or *cimborio*, which has a pointed roof flanked by small round turrets. These roofs are all covered with tilelike slabs laid one over the other like the scales of a pine cone, a practice common at the same time in the Poitou and Limousin regions of France. In the sixteenth century the new cathedral was enlarged by encroaching on the old one, as can be seen on the very right of the illustration above.

Façade, church of Santo Domingo, Soria. Twelfth century ▶

Among the finest and largest cloisters of the period are those at Santo Domingo de Silos. Sculpture appears not only on the bells of the capitals but also in large low reliefs on the corner piers of the passageway. On the latter are scenes from the life of Christ, such as the Ascension depicted here. It is possible to make out in these sculptures the activity of different workshops, one more recent and more highly developed technically than the other but, at the same time, less gifted with creative imagination. Some scholars have suggested that the sculpture here, in particular the low reliefs with their expressive faces and their draperies in broken folds, is not unlike that done at about the same time at Moissac and Souillac in the Languedoc region. Be that as it may, this is one of the most splendid ensembles in Spain.

Cloister of the monastery of Santo Domingo de Silos (Burgos). Late-eleventh–twelfth centuries

The old city of Soria still has many important Romanesque buildings. The façade of Santo Domingo, which is towerless and wider than it is high, is reminiscent of some buildings in the west of France, with its blind arcades and rose window framed by several concentric sculptured moldings. The portal has multiple archivolts, on which a swarm of tiny Biblical figures are vigorously sculpted in high relief. The relief on the tympanum has a typical Spanish motif: the Trinity with God the Father holding the Son on His lap.

◀ Tribune in the church of Serrabone (Pyrénées-Orientales). Mid-twelfth century. Rose marble, width 18′ 4″, depth 15′ 9″.

ROMANESQUE ARCHITECTURE IN PORTUGAL

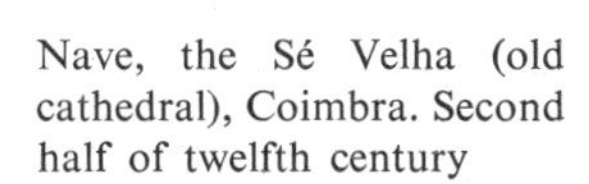

Nave, the Sé Velha (old cathedral), Coimbra. Second half of twelfth century

Portugal carried on very active and regular relationships with the other Christian countries of the West, and its art—as the cathedral at Coimbra proves—did not develop in isolation. The elevation of the nave appears to be directly imitated from that of Sainte-Foy in Conques: the same great compound articulation of the nave arcades, twinned arches opening onto the galleries above, tunnel vaulting with transverse arches, and a lantern tower over the crossing. The cathedral was built about 1170 by the master masons Bernard and Robert, the latter of whom was probably French.

◀ The Roussillon region of France has many of the characteristics of neighboring Catalonia, of which it originally formed a part. The old priory church of Serrabone, perched on a mountain, has in the middle of its nave a curious tribune, or raised gallery, which is completely covered with carving in very low relief of great decorative effect and real delicacy of execution. The motifs are not merely ornamental but include angels, people, and those fabulous animals which belong to the mysterious, bewitching world of Romanesque art. The tribune, it seems, is no longer in its original position in the church.

Rotunda of the Knights Templars in the Convento do Cristo, Tomar (Santarem). Second half of twelfth century

For their monastery at Tomar, the Knights Templars constructed an edifice on a central-plan design inspired by the Temple of Jerusalem, and it is the most remarkable and best-preserved example of this curious type of structure to survive. The rotunda is in the form of an octagonal prism with a central sanctuary and a sixteen-sided ambulatory. Such central-plan churches are frequent in Asia Minor and wherever Byzantine art exerted its influence. In the West they are found chiefly in the Germanic regions, but also in Spain and Italy. Here the form was adopted by the Templars for symbolic reasons. In the sixteenth century, King Manoel added decoration to it and linked it up with a nave, so that, as it stands today, the rotunda serves as the choir of a church.

CHRONOLOGICAL TABLES

I. Architecture in the Romanesque Era

980 990 1000 1010 1020 1030 1040 1050 1060 1070 1080 1090

France

1025 Poitiers, St.-Hilaire, begun
c. 1060 Caen, St.-Étienne, begu
1060–1115 St.-Savin-sur-Garten
981 Cluny,
second abbey church
?c. 1060 Toulouse, St.-Sernin, be
1005–1049 Reims, St.-Remi
c. 1040–1067 Jumièges, abbey
1019 Tournus, St.-Philibert, first consecration
St.-Benoît-

Germany

1025 Limburg an der Hardt begun
c. 1030 Speyer, cathedral, begun
1016–1047 Trier, cathedral, west front
c. 1040 Cologne, St. Maria im Kapitol, begun
1009–1243 Mainz, cathedral
1071 Hirsau, St. Aure
1001–1033 Hildesheim, St. Michael

Italy

1066 Monte Cassino,
abbey, rebuilding begu
Pomposa, abbey
c. 1075 S. Angel
c. 1060–1150 Florence, baptiste
c. 1062 Florence, S. Miniato,
interior completed
1063–1095 Como, S. Abbond
1063–1350 Pisa, cathedral grc

Spain and Portugal

1020–1032 Ripoll, monastery
1022 S. Pedro de Roda consecrated
Sto. Domingo
1090 Á
Loa

England and the Low Countries

Maastri
1079–1090 Winche
1083
1c
Tour

History

987–1328 Capetian kings
1046 Norman domination in Apulia
1024–1125 Salic emperors
1066 Norman conquest of Eng
11th–13th centuries Reconquest of Spain
1075 Dispute

980 990 1000 1010 1020 1030 1040 1050 1060 1070 1080 1090

o 1110 1120 1130 1140 1150 1160 1170 1180 1190 1200 1210 1220 1230 1240 1250

Paray-le-Monial, abbey c. 1135–1144 St.-Denis, cathedral
Conques, Ste.-Foy
c. 1100 Cluny, third abbey church

Laon, cathedral
1115 Clairvaux founded Arles, St.-Trophime
c. 1120 Autun, cathedral, begun
ire begun 1120 Vézelay, La Madeleine, begun 1164 Sens, cathedral, consecrated
c. 1150 Bayeux, cathedral
Poitiers, Notre-Dame c. 1170 St.-Gilles-du-Gard, façade

---

aria Laach, abbey, begun
1103–1140 Lund (Sweden), cathedral

npleted Prüfening, St. Georg
1200–1220 Soest, St. Patroklus
1133–1172 Hildesheim, St. Godehard Limburg an der Lahn, St. Georg
Jerichow, monastery church
Cologne, Church of the Apostles, apse

---

9 Modena, cathedral, begun 1131 Cefalù, cathedral, begun 1174 Monreale, cathedral, begun
1173 Pisa, campanile, begun
c. 1128 Milan, S. Ambrogio, nave
mis completed Palermo, S. Cataldo
1112–1147 Lucca, S. Frediano
1139 Parma, cathedral, begun
Pavia, S. Michele
1125–1178 Verona, S. Zeno Maggiore
1172 Palermo, cathedral, begun

---

s, monastery 1123 Tahull, S. Clemente, consecrated Tomar, Convento do Cristo Sahagún, S. Lorenzo
walls, begun Santiago de Compostela Coimbra, old cathedral Poblet, monastery Lérida, old cathedral
tle León, S. Isidoro 1152 Salamanca, old cathedral, begun

---

ze Lieve Vrouwekerk
hedral 1118 Peterborough, cathedral, begun
hedral, begun c. 1140 Fountains Abbey
3 Durham, cathedral
hedral 1175–1178 Canterbury, cathedral, choir

---

99 Crusaders seize Jerusalem 1138–1254 Hohenstaufen emperors
98 Cistercian Order founded 1130–1154 Roger II, Norman King of Sicily
estiture 1115 St. Bernard founds Clairvaux
Cid conquers Valencia 1151 Death of Abbot Suger of St.-Denis
1122 Concordat of Worms 1154 Plantagenets in England

o 1110 1120 1130 1140 1150 1160 1170 1180 1190 1200 1210 1220 1230 1240 1250

II. Painting and Sculpture in the Romanesque Era

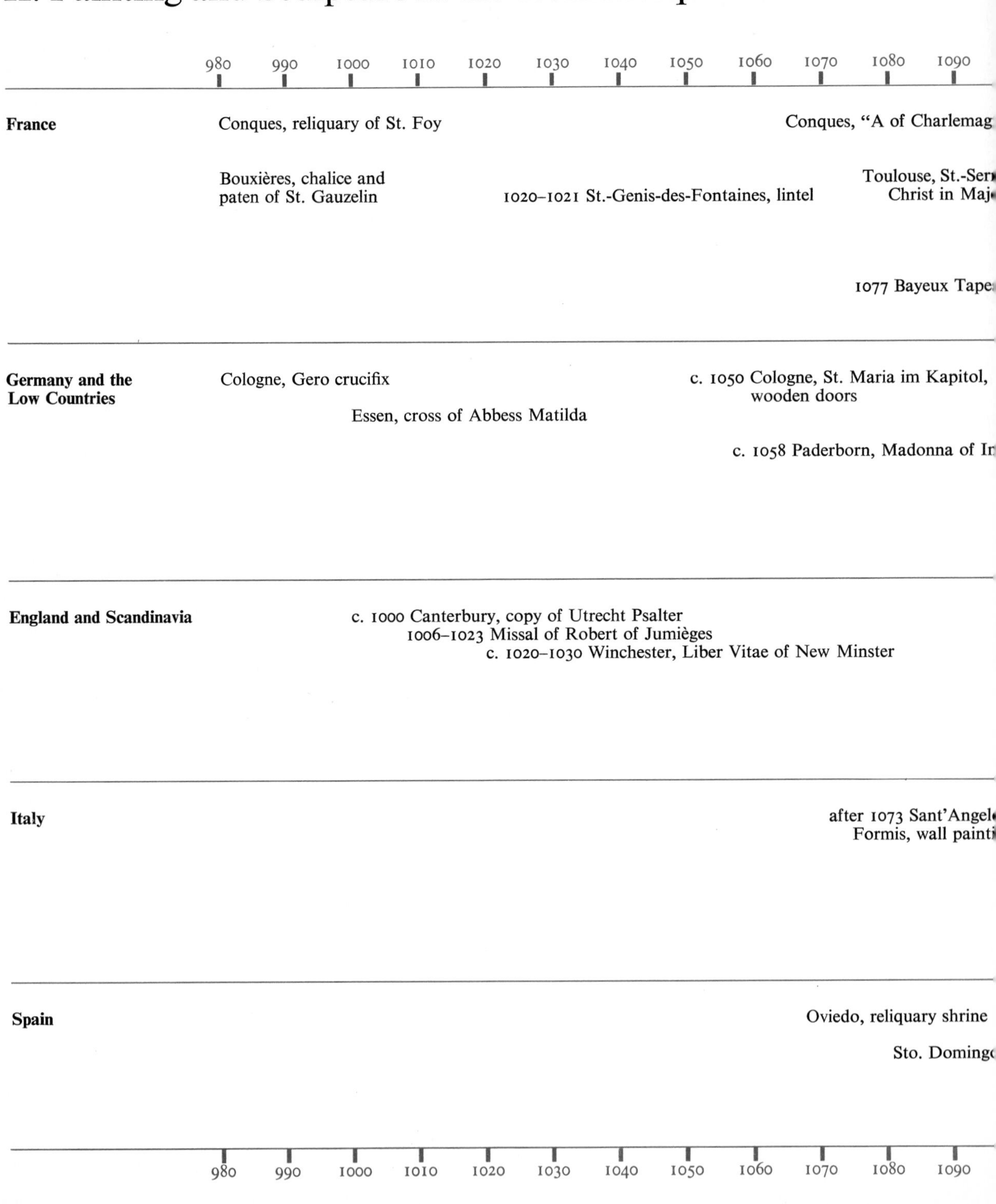

0 1110 1120 1130 1140 1150 1160 1170 1180 1190 1200 1210 1220 1230 1240 1250

. 1100 St.-Savin-sur-Gartempe, frescoes in porch
c. 1187 Nazareth (Israel), basilica, capitals
c. 1125–1135 Autun, cathedral, reliefs by Gislebertus
Cluny, capitals
c. 1110 Toulouse, St.-Sernin, Porte Miégeville
Vézelay, capitals
Arles, St.-Trophime, façade
Conques, tympanum
Souillac, bestiary pillar
St.-Gilles-du-Gard, porch
c. 1145 Chartres, westwork, begun

:. 1100 Rogerus of Helmarshausen
c. 1150 Alpirsbach, lectern in Freudenstadt
:. 1100 Gernrode, Entombment
Prüfening, frescoes
Freiberg, St. Maria, Golden Portal
1107–1118 Liège (Belgium), St.-Barthélemy, baptismal font
1170–1180 Hochelten, reliquary
c. 1115 Externsteine, stone reliefs
Novgorod (Russia), bronze doors
1129 Freckenhorst, baptismal font
Maria Laach, tomb slab of Abbot Gilbertus
1133–1172 Hildesheim, St. Godehard, capitals
c. 1188 Soest, altar frontal
1170–1200 Basel (Switzerland), cathedral, St. Gall portal
Stavelot, reliquary triptych
doc. 1181–1205 Nicholas of Verdun
Brunswick, crucifix of Imerward
c. 1220–1230 Hildesheim, baptismal font

---

c. 1110 Gloucester, candlestick
Mosjö, Madonna
c. 1115–1125 Canterbury, cathedral, capitals in crypt
c. 1200–1210 Wells, tomb of Bishop Levericus
c. 1140 Ely, cathedral, Prior's Door
c. 1140 Lisbjerg, Golden Altar
Bury St. Edmunds, Bury Bible
c. 1150 Canterbury, Lambeth Bible
c. 1150 Canterbury, Eadwine Psalter
Chichester, cathedral, stone reliefs
c. 1155–1165 Malmesbury, abbey, tympanum
c. 1160 Winchester Bible

1098 Bari, episcopal throne
Pavia, S. Michele, façade reliefs
:. 1100 Verona, S. Zeno Maggiore, bronze doors
c. 1150–c. 1225 Benedetto Antelami
Palermo, tomb of Frederick II
fl. c. 1170–1180 Barisano of Trani
fl. c. 1173–c. 1200 Bonanno Pisano
c. 1175 Salerno, cathedral, ambo
Monreale, cathedral, capitals in cloister
Parma, baptistery, sculpture
Spoleto, S. Pietro, façade

:. 1100 Bible of Ripoll
? 1157–1188 León, S. Isidoro, wall paintings in the Royal Pantheon
1123 Tahull, S. Clemente, apse painting
Tarrasa, Sta. Maria, wall paintings
os, capitals
Ripoll, monastery, façade
Majestad Battló
Santiago de Compostela, Puerta de las Platerías
Sto. Domingo de Silos, altar frontal
Lérida, Porta dels Fillols

00 1110 1120 1130 1140 1150 1160 1170 1180 1190 1200 1210 1220 1230 1240 1250

Bibliography

Only a brief selection of suggestions can be given here. A number of works in foreign languages have been included, either because their subjects have not been treated in English or because they have excellent and numerous photographs.

CULTURAL BACKGROUND

BALDWIN, M. W., *The Mediaeval Church*, Ithaca, N. Y., 1953

BOISSONNADE, P., *Life and Work in Medieval Europe*, New York, 1964

COPLESTON, F., *A History of Philosophy*, Vol. 2, *Medieval Philosophy*, Pt. I, New York, 1962

EVANS, J., *Monastic Life at Cluny, 910–1157*, London, 1931

HOYT, R. S., ed., *Life and Thought in the Early Middle Ages*, Minneapolis, 1967

KANTOROWICZ, E. H., *The King's Two Bodies: A Study of Medieval Political Theology*, Princeton, 1957

RUNCIMAN, S., *A History of the Crusades*, New York, 1951–54, 3 vols.

TAYLOR, H. O., *The Mediaeval Mind: A History of the Development of Thought and Emotion in the Middle Ages*, 4th ed., Cambridge, Mass., 1959, 2 vols.

VIELLIARD, J., ed., *Le Guide du pèlerin de Saint-Jacques de Compostelle*, Paris, 1950

GENERAL

AINAUD, J., *Romanesque Painting*, New York, 1963

ANTHONY, E. W., *Romanesque Frescoes*, Princeton, 1951

BALTRUŠAITIS, J., *Le Stylistique ornemental dans la sculpture romane*, Paris, 1931

CLAPHAM, A. W., *Romanesque Architecture in Western Europe*, New York, 1936

CONANT, K. J., *Carolingian and Romanesque Architecture: 800–1200*, Baltimore, 1959

CROZET, R., *L'Art roman*, Paris, 1962

DIRINGER, D., *The Illuminated Book, Its History and Production*, Boston, 1958

EGBERT, V., ed., *The Mediaeval Artist at Work*, Princeton, 1967

El Arte romanico, exhibition catalogue, Barcelona and Santiago de Compostela, 1961

EVANS, J., *Cluniac Art of the Romanesque Period*, Cambridge, England, 1950

EVANS, J., *The Romanesque Architecture of the Order of Cluny*, Cambridge, England, 1938

FOCILLON, H., *L'Art des sculpteurs romans*, Paris, 1931

FOCILLON, H., *The Art of the West in the Middle Ages*, Vol. I, *Romanesque Art*, Greenwich, Conn., 1963

GRABAR, A., and NORDENFALK, C., *Romanesque Painting*, New York, 1958

HOLT, E. G., ed., *A Documentary History of Art*, Vol. I, *The Middle Ages and the Renaissance*, Garden City, N. Y., 1957

MOREY, C. R., *Medieval Art*, New York, 1942

PORTER, A. K., *Medieval Architecture*, New Haven, 1912, 2 vols.

PORTER, A. K., *Romanesque Sculpture of the Pilgrimage Roads*, New York, 1966, 3 vols.

THEOPHILUS, *On Divers Arts*, ed. and trans. J. C. Hawthorne and C. S. Smith, Chicago, 1963

TOY, S., *A History of Fortification*, Chester Springs, Pa., 1954

FRANCE

AUBERT, M., and COUBET, S., *Romanesque Cathedrals and Abbeys of France*, New York, 1966

CHAPLET, B., *Auvergne romane* (Zodiaque), La Pierre-qui-Vire, 1962

DEBIDOUR, V. H., *Le Bestiaire sculpté du moyen âge en France*, Paris, 1961

DESCHAMPS, P., *French Sculpture of the Romanesque Period*, Florence, 1930

DESCHAMPS, P., and THIBOUT, M., *La Peinture murale en France*, Paris, 1963

DESCHAMPS, P., and THIBOUT, M., *La Peinture romane en France, le haut moyen âge et l'époque romane*, Paris, 1951

DIMIER, A., and PORCHER, J., *L'Art cistercien* (Zodiaque), La Pierre-qui-Vire, 1962

EVANS, J., *Art in Mediaeval France, 987–1498*, New York, 1948

FOCILLON, H., *Peintures romanes des églises de France*, Paris, 1938

GAILLARD, G., et al., *Rouergue roman* (Zodiaque), La Pierre-qui-Vire, 1963

GANTNER, J., and POBÉ, M., *Romanesque Art in France*, London, 1956

GRIVOT, D., and ZARNECKI, G., *Gislebertus, Sculptor of Autun*, New York, 1961

GRODECKI, L., *The Stained Glass of French Churches*, London, 1948

HUBERT, J., *L'Architecture religieuse du haut moyen âge en France*, Paris, 1952

MAURY, J., et al., *Limousin roman* (Zodiaque), La Pierre-qui-Vire, 1960

PORCHER, J., *Medieval French Miniatures*, New York, 1959

Trésors des Églises de France, exhibition catalogue, Paris, 1965

VIDAL, M., et al., *Quercy roman* (Zodiaque), La Pierre-qui-Vire, 1959

WIXOM, W. D., *Treasures from Medieval France*, Cleveland, 1967

ENGLAND

BOASE, T. S. R., *English Art, 1100–1216*, New York, 1953

CLAPHAM, A. W., *English Romanesque Architecture*, New York, 1930–34, 2 vols.

MILLAR, E. G., *English Illuminated Manuscripts*, Paris, 1926

RICE, D. T., *English Art, 871–1100*, New York, 1952

RICKERT, M., *Painting in Britain: The Middle Ages*, Baltimore, 1956

STENTON, F. M., ed., *The Bayeux Tapestry*, 2nd ed., Greenwich, Conn., 1965

WEBB, G., *Architecture in Britain: The Middle Ages*, Baltimore, 1956

ZARNECKI G. *English Romanesque Sculpture*, London, 1951–53, 2 vols.

NORTHERN COUNTRIES

BEENKEN, H. T., *Romanische Skulptur in Deutschland (11. und 12. Jahrhundert)*, Leipzig, 1924

BRAUN, J., *Meisterwerke der Deutschen Goldschmiedekunst der Vorgotischen Zeit*, Munich, 1922, 2 vols.

BUSCH, H., *Germania romanica*, Vienna, 1963

COLLON-GEVAERT, S., et al., *Art roman dans la vallée de la Meuse aux XIe et XIIe siècles*, Brussels, 1962

GALL, E., *Cathedrals and Abbey Churches of the Rhine*, New York, 1963

GOLDSCHMIDT, A., *German Illumination*, Florence, 1928

HAHR, A., *Architecture in Sweden*, Stockholm, 1938

HENZE, A., *Westfälische Kunstgeschichte*, Recklinghausen, 1957

LEMAIRE, R., *De Romaanse Bouwkunst in de Nederlanden*, Brussels, 1952

MACKEPRANG, M., and JENSEN, C., *Danish Churches*, Copenhagen, 1940–

Romanische Kunst in Österreich, exhibition catalogue, Krems an der Donau, 1964

SWARZENSKI, H., *Monuments of Romanesque Art*, London, 1954

WILL, R., *Alsace romane* (Zodiaque), La Pierre-qui-Vire, 1965

ITALY

ANTHONY, E. W., *Early Florentine Architecture and Decoration*, Cambridge, Mass., 1927

BOSSAGLIA R., *Scultura italiana dell'alto medioevo all'età romanica*, Milan, 1966

CRICHTON, G. H., *Romanesque Sculpture in Italy*, London, 1954

DECKER, H., *Romanesque Art in Italy*, New York, 1959

DE FRANKOVICH, G., *Benedetto Antelami, architetto e scultore, e l'arte del suo tempo*, Milan, 1952

DEMUS, O., *The Mosaics of Norman Sicily*, London, 1950

DI STEFANO, G., *Monumenti della Sicilia normanna*, Palermo, 1955

GARRISON, E. B., *Italian Romanesque Panel Painting*, Florence, 1949

GOZZOLA, P., *San Zeno, Bible des Pauvres: Porte de bronze de Vérone*, Lausanne, 1956

HUTTON, E., *The Cosmati*, London, 1950

PORTER, A. K., *Lombard Architecture*, New Haven, 1915–17, 4 vols.

RICCI, C., *Romanesque Architecture in Italy*, New York, 1925

SALMI, M., *Italian Miniatures*, New York, 1954

SALMI, M., *L'Architettura romanica in Toscana*, Milan, 1928

SALMI, M., *Romanesque Sculpture in Tuscany*, Florence, 1928

SALVINI, R., *Il Chiostro di Monreale e la scultura romanica in Sicilia*, Palermo, 1962

SALVINI, R., *Wiligelmo e le origini della scultura romanica*, Milan, 1956

WILLEMSEN, C. A., and ODENTHAL, D., *Puglia, Terra dei Normanni e degli Svevi*, Bari, 1959

SPAIN

CONANT, K. J., *The Early Architectural History of the Cathedral of Santiago de Compostela*, Cambridge, Mass., 1926

COOK, W. W. S., and GUDIOL RICART, J., *Pintura e Imagineria románicas* (Ars Hispaniae VI), Madrid, 1950

DURLIAT, M., *Roussillon roman* (Zodiaque), La Pierre-qui-Vire, 1964

HILDBURGH, W. L., *Medieval Spanish Enamels*, London, 1936

JUNYENT, E., *Catalogne romane* (Zodiaque), La Pierre-qui-Vire, 1960–61, 2 vols.

LOJENDIO, L. M. DE, *Navarre romane* (Zodiaque), La Pierre-qui-Vire, 1967

PALOL, P. DE, and HIRMER, M., *Early Medieval Art in Spain*, New York, 1966

PORTER, A. K., *Spanish Romanesque Sculpture*, Florence, 1928, 2 vols.

RICART, J. C., and GAYA NUÑO, J. A., *Arquitectura y escultura románicas* (Ars Hispaniae V), Madrid, 1948

RODRÍGUEZ, A., and LOJENDIO, L. M. DE, *Castille romane* (Zodiaque), La Pierre-qui-Vire, 1966

WHITEHALL, W. H., *Spanish Romanesque Architecture of the Eleventh Century*, London, 1941

Index